Slow Cook
Fast Food

Visit our How To website at www.howto.co.uk

At **www.howto.co.uk** you can engage in conversation with our authors – all of whom have 'been there and done that' in their specialist fields. You can get access to special offers and additional content, but most importantly you will be able to engage with, and become a part of, a wide and growing community of people just like yourself.

At **www.howto.co.uk** you'll be able to talk and share tips with people who have similar interests and are facing similar challenges in their lives. People who, just like you, have the desire to change their lives for the better – be it through moving to a new country, starting a new business, growing their own vegetables, or writing a novel.

At **www.howto.co.uk** you'll find the support and encouragement you need to help make your aspirations a reality.

You can go direct to www.slow-cook-fast-food.co.uk, which is part of the main How To site.

How To Books strives to present authentic, inspiring, practical information in its books. Now, when you buy a title from **How To Books,** you get even more than just words on a page.

Slow Cook
Fast Food

Over 250 healthy, wholesome slow cooker
and one pot meals for all the family

SARAH FLOWER

SPRING HILL

Published by Spring Hill, an imprint of How To Books Ltd.
Spring Hill House, Spring Hill Road
Begbroke, Oxford OX5 1RX
United Kingdom
Tel: (01865) 375794
Fax: (01865) 379162
info@howtobooks.co.uk
www.howtobooks.co.uk

How To Books greatly reduce the carbon footprint of their books
by sourcing their typesetting and printing in the UK.

Text © 2010 Sarah Flower
Photographs © 2010 www.fabfoodpix.com

British Library Cataloguing in Publication Data
A catalogue record of this book is available from the British Library.

ISBN: 978 1 905862 41 2

Produced for How To Books by Deer Park Productions, Tavistock, Devon
Designed and typeset by Mousemat Design Ltd
Edited by Jennifer Gregory
Printed and bound by in Great Britain by Bell & Bain Ltd, Glasgow

NOTE: The material contained in this book is set out in good faith for general guidance and no
liability can be accepted for loss or expense incurred as a result of relying in particular circumstances
on statements made in the book. Laws and regulations are complex and liable to change, and readers
should check the current position with relevant authorities before making personal arrangements.

Contents

To my wonderful family for enduring the cooking experiments, calming my bad moods and keeping me topped up with tea and chocolate. A huge thanks to my mum who has helped me with many of the recipes in this book and for giving me the skills and passion for cooking.

Introduction

Slow Cook Fast Food sounds like a complete contradiction in terms, but those used to one pot and slow cooker dishes will understand my reasoning. It is really no surprise why one pot and slow cooker recipes are making such a comeback. In our busy world we want healthy food and fast food but, sadly, the two don't always go hand in hand. Yet with one pot meals and, in particular, with the help of a slow cooker, you really can have a healthy, nutritious, instant meal waiting for you when you come home after a busy day.

This book is packed with traditional and new recipes gathered from friends and family. There is a wide variety to choose from, including many vegetarian and vegan options. I have enjoyed experimenting and I hope you enjoy the results.

The joy of slow cook
Our desire to create thrifty, wholesome meals has seen a resurrection for the slow cooker – and about time too, in my opinion!

The key to creating successful slow cooker dishes is to be organised. Slow cook meals *must* be planned in advance – there is no point in coming home after a busy day and then thinking of putting something in the slow cooker. In most cases you will need to prepare the food in the morning or the night before. Don't panic, this doesn't have to be as arduous as it sounds. You should only need to spend 15–30 minutes maximum in preparation and you will be rewarded with a wonderfully nutritious hot meal waiting for you when you come home from work.

I love the simplicity of the slow cooker. You fill it with your ingredients (no need to sauté, brown off or similar unless you want to brown the meat), pop the lid on and walk away for 6–10 hours depending on the setting. Because, as its name suggests, the slow cooker cooks slowly, and the nutrients are preserved. Another bonus of cooking food slowly is that it won't spoil if you want to delay dinner for half an hour – invaluable if, as happens in our house, everyone seems to call just as I am about to serve a meal.

For those of us concerned about saving money, the slow cooker is ideal. Manufacturers claim it uses no more electricity than a light bulb and you can fill it with cheaper cuts of meat which, when cooked slowly, produce tender and tasty dishes. You can also make delicious soups, puddings and even conserves and chutneys. I must confess, making chutney brings out the domestic goddess in me. There is something magical about using up any unwanted ingredients and creating something special. I just wish I had a Victorian-style pantry to keep them all in.

Enjoy experimenting with your slow cooker. I have, by trial and error, perfected cakes, sponge puddings and delicious mugs of hot chocolate brownies. And don't forget your slow cooker at Christmas; you can steam the Christmas pudding, prepare mulled wine and cook your gammon joint. Any leftover turkey can be turned into a delicious casserole, leaving you time to sit back, relax and enjoy Christmas.

The joy of one pot

One pot dishes really do mean what they say – a dish that is served in one pot. This could be something simple like shepherd's pie, or a hob dish such as a stir-fry, or even a curry. Why not put together one large serving dish of salad, enabling everyone simply to dig in and enjoy? There are no hard and fast rules. I am a great believer in simple food that does not require a degree in home economics or specialist equipment to prepare.

Some of the recipes do involve using more than one pot or utensil in order to create them – this may seem like a cheat but I have it on good authority that one pot dishes are really about serving in one pot and not the work that goes on behind the scenes.

Take pride in serving meals. Food should look good as well as taste good – it is a creative manifestation of your affection for those sharing your meal. I collect ovenproof dishes – particularly earthenware, which I love; there is something really rustic and wholesome about setting a table with a selection of one pot dishes served in earthenware pots. If you are catering for a group of friends or family, why not experiment with lots of little dishes of varying colours and flavours instead of one big dish?

I hope you enjoy this book and it inspires you to create your own recipes. Good luck!

One Pot and Slow Cook Cooking: Equipment and Advice

As with any trade, you need the right tools to create good work, but that doesn't mean you have to spend lots of money. With each recipe you will find a list of the equipment required. Here is a brief summary of the items you will need.

Slow cooker
Casserole dish
Ovenproof dish
Wok
Sauté pan
Serving dish
Roasting tin

The Slow Cooker

Slow cookers gained popularity in the 1970s with their promise of a wholesome, economical meal ready for the family's return after a busy day. Sadly they became relegated to kitchen cupboards as we moved into the Thatcher years of 'loads of money' when for many people the need for frugality was less relevant. Cheaper cuts of meats became less popular so there seemed to be no real reason to keep the slow cooker in our kitchens. The microwave and processed food became the housewife's choice for a busy home and the poor slow cooker ceased to inspire. Thankfully we are now seeing its revival as we realise that this clever machine can not only save us time, but also create meals that are superior nutritionally.

You can buy slow cookers from as little as £15 from your supermarket, electrical store or Argos. See the chapter 'Contacts and Further Information' for more details on specific models plus contact details for manufacturers and retailers. If you are a member of Freecycle, you may find someone is giving one away, or you could put out a 'Wanted' request. Boot sales are also a great place for picking up a bargain. I have a Crock-Pot and a stainless steel slow cooker. I know it sounds extravagant, but sometimes I am cooking two dishes at the same time, either a dessert and a main meal, or two main meals if I am trying to get ahead or use up fresh ingredients.

To sauté or not to sauté

Recipes often tell you to sauté the onions or brown the meat. I have tried with and without and to be honest I really did not notice much difference in the taste, just colour sometimes. If you are cooking a whole chicken, for example, remember that this will not brown, so may look a bit unappealing. You can coat the meat with a sauce or marinade to make it look more appetising, or you can brown this before or after the slow cook. If you prefer to brown your meat or fry your onions before placing in the slow cooker, you can use your hob. Some slow cookers have a sauté facility; others come with hob-proof dishes, allowing you to transfer from one source to the other. You will need to refer to your manufacturer's instructions for more information. As I am trying to cater for those with and without slow cookers, I have kept the sauté option within the recipe – it is up to you to decide if you want to do this or not.

Slow cooking techniques

All slow cookers will come with full instructions and may even include some recipe ideas. Here are some reminders:

Some cookers need to be preheated, which can take up to 15 minutes; others heat up fast so you may not need to do this (refer to your manufacturer's recommendations). As a general rule of thumb, one hour in a conventional oven equates to 2–3 hours on high in a slow cooker, or 6 hours on low heat. If I am making a stew or casserole, I do take the easy route and just add the ingredients and leave it to do its own thing.

The key point to remember about slow cooking is that once you set it off cooking, you shouldn't keep removing the lid. This reduces the temperature and then it takes longer for the slow cooker to get back up to the required temperature. Only remove it when absolutely necessary – ideally just when it finishes cooking. If you are the sort of person who likes to keep an eye on things, opt for a slow cooker with a glass lid (though this is not foolproof as they can get steamed up!).

Always defrost any frozen ingredients thoroughly before placing them in the slow cooker, especially meat. The slow cooker is designed to cook safely at low temperatures; however, if your cooker does not maintain the required heat, this could increase the risk of food poisoning caused by the spread of bacteria.

When adding liquids such as stock or water, to maintain the temperature it is better to use warm liquids (not boiling) rather than cold.

Vegetables, particularly root vegetables, take the longest time to cook.

Seafood, dairy and frozen vegetables only need to be added in the last half hour or hour of cooking.

Fresh herbs can lose their flavour so it is often best to use dried herbs and only add fresh herbs in the last half an hour of cooking time.

Your slow cooker should come with an instruction booklet which can explain this in more detail.

Cakes

I have made cakes in the slow cooker and these have been really tasty, though sometimes they can be a different texture from oven-baked. I think this is a matter of personal taste: some people may not like the moist, almost bread pudding type texture of the fruit cakes. I have cooked cakes simply by placing the cake dish in the slow cooker and I have also added water to the base, creating a bain-marie. This works well with sponge puddings and Christmas pudding.

Alcohol

You may notice that some recipes in this book include alcohol. If you are worried about giving this to children, don't be as it does burn off during cooking and just leaves the flavour. If you are still concerned, you can use alcohol-free wines, which are great if you like the flavour but can give you extra peace of mind, or simply exclude wine from the recipe.

One Pot

One pot presentation

The beauty of most one pot dishes is in the final presentation – serving one pot dishes has a wonderful wholesome quality about it. Below is a list of one pot equipment.

Ovenproof dishes

I am a big fan of Pyrex dishes. They seem to last for years and are relatively cheap to buy (and available from most supermarkets). I have a few in different sizes. They are ideal for lasagnes, crumbles and a variety of other one pot dishes. Pyrex make an amazing casserole dish that can tolerate extreme temperatures – you can take it straight from the freezer and place it in the oven or on a hob without fear of it shattering.

Casserole dishes

Le Creuset has some fabulous casserole dishes which will all work well on hobs. If you like the style but not the price, you could try to locate them second-hand. JML recently launched their Country Cookware which looks just like the Le Creuset range but is half the price. It also comes with a 25-year guarantee. Visit www.jmldirect.co.uk for more information.

Saucepans

Saucepans can seem expensive, but if you buy well they will last for years. Look upon their purchase as an investment. I have bought cheap pans in the past, but within a year the handles fall off or the bases have been marked. In my experience the thicker the pan base, the better the results. These pans retain heat, enabling you to cook at lower temperatures, ultimately saving you electricity. To avoid nasty accidents make sure the lids fit securely and the handles are firmly attached. Avoid aluminium pans as some research has shown a link to diseases such as Alzheimer's and even breast cancer.

I use a set of four stainless steel pans for normal saucepan duties. All my pans can also be placed in the oven; this means they can be used for a multitude of meals, such as frittatas which start off on the hob before being placed in a medium hot oven to cook.

Sauté, wok and frying pans

I have a Le Creuset 30 cm sauté pan which I adore. It is perfect for making sauces and quick meals such as Spaghetti Bolognese, curries and pasta sauces. I also have a wok for stir-fries and a small frying pan.

Steamer

If you are serious about cooking food that's both healthy and tasty you really must invest in a steamer. You can buy stainless steel steamers that sit on the hob or simple electric steamers. Steaming avoids vitamin loss and to my mind enhances the taste of the vegetables. I never boil vegetables – not even for roast potatoes – I steam instead of parboil. Electric steamers have an amazing way of keeping the vegetables warm when cooked, without risk of them continuing to cook and go soggy – not sure how this is done but it is fantastic.

Roasting tin
You can place a joint of meat and vegetables in one roasting tin, for a simple one pot dish. I have three different sizes; two are non-stick tins, the other a Pyrex roasting dish. If you are cooking for a large family, you may have to use two dishes instead of one.

The electric hand blender
This is also known as a stick blender. I prefer using an electric hand blender rather than a liquidiser. I use my hand blender for a variety of tasks: I make smoothies, purée soups, and – using the attachments – I can chop herbs, onions and other foods in seconds. You can buy electric hand blenders for as little as £4, but if you pay a bit more, you can buy one with chopping attachments and even some with balloon whisks.

Mixing bowls
Mixing bowls are essential for any kitchen. Great for mixing, soaking and whisking, they can even double up as serving bowls if necessary. I personally prefer ceramic or stainless steel as I find plastic too flimsy, but it is a personal choice.

Electric mixer
If you haven't already got an electric mixer or an electric hand blender, why not opt for a machine that does both? Electric hand blenders can come with balloon whisk attachments. Alternatively you can buy a great little mixer for less than £5 from large supermarkets or Argos. They are good for making cakes, pancakes or whisking egg whites, but I also use mine for fluffing up mashed potato. I am a bit of a collector of food mixers. I love the style of the 1950s and have two Sunbeam food mixers – one chrome and one white Bakelite. On a daily basis though, I use my 1970s large Kenwood – my pride and joy which I paid £10 for from a local boot sale!

Serving dishes
These are ideal for all meals, whether pasta, salad or even a dessert. It's handy to have

a variety of serving dishes, especially when you are entertaining. Boot sales are great places to pick up kitchen items; you can often find earthenware and decorative serving dishes for very little.

So, now you have got your kitchen in order, it's time to experiment with the recipes. I hope you enjoy them. I have designed each recipe to feed a family of four.

Weights, Temperature and Measures

I am constantly being asked for the recipes for my cakes and it always throws me into turmoil as I never measure anything when baking. My husband laughs as he sees me literally throwing in all sorts of ingredients, seemingly oblivious to the end result. Thankfully they all come out perfectly yummy!

Don't follow my lead – until you are confident, measure as you go. There is some great measuring equipment available to make life easier.

Measuring spoons
You can buy a neat little set of measuring spoons for around £2. They are ideal for recipes that need teaspoon, tablespoon or dessertspoon measurements.

Measuring cups
These are good for measuring dry ingredients or liquids. Some show measures for key ingredients such as flour or sugar, others just measure in millilitres.

Measuring jug
I use a glass Pyrex measuring jug. They are very hardy and come up gleaming after every wash – unlike plastic jugs which can stain. Measuring jugs are ideal for measuring liquids or mixing ingredients together. I also have a great Pyrex measuring jug which shows grams for sugar, flour and mixed fruit. I have picked up various pieces of kitchenalia from boot sales and auctions over the years.

Scales
Find a set of scales that suits your kitchen. I like the retro-looking scales with a deep bowl which is ideal for weighing a variety of ingredients. Scales can cost as little as £3 to buy new.

Weights table

1 ounce is equal to approximately 28g, but for ease of use, most tables round down to 25g per ounce and gradually increase this as the weight increases. See the table below for clarity.

WEIGHT		LIQUID MEASURE	
Metric (approx.)	Imperial	Metric (approx.)	Imperial
25–30g	1oz	5ml	1 teaspoon (tsp)
50–55g	2oz	15ml	1 tablespoon (tbsp)
85g	3oz	25–30ml	1 fl oz
100g	3.5oz	50ml	2 fl oz
125g	4oz	75ml	3 fl oz
150g	5oz	100–125ml	4 fl oz
175g	6oz	150ml	5 fl oz
200g	7oz	175ml	6 fl oz
225g	8oz	200ml	7 fl oz
250g	9oz	225ml	8 fl oz
280g	10oz	250ml	9 fl oz
350g	12oz	300ml	10 fl oz (½ pint)
400g	14oz	600ml	20 fl oz (1 pint)
450g	16oz/1lb	1 litre	1¾ pints
900kg	2lb		

Oven temperatures

Oven temperatures recommended in recipes are for a preheated oven – this means the oven needs to have reached the recommended temperature before you put the food in. Fan-assisted ovens may cook faster, so I always lower the recommended temperature slightly.

All the recipes are designed to feed a family of four.

One Pot Soups

Soups are bursting with nutrients. Quick and easy, they can be used as an instant snack or a nutritious meal; they are cheap too! Kids can be tempted with a side helping of toasted soldiers, hot pitta bread with hummus or even healthy potato wedges. If you or your child has a packed lunch, why not invest in a small flask and fill it with your home-made soup – satisfying and warming, especially during the winter months.

Tips for making soup

- **Stock** – I don't use stock cubes; they are far too salty and totally overpower the natural flavours. Instead I just add water or I make a vegetable stock. If you prefer to make your own fresh stock, see Essentials on page 184 for more information.
- **Puréeing soups** – some people like a chunky soup, others prefer a smooth one. It is purely personal taste. When puréeing soup, I use an electric hand blender (also known as a stick blender). It is simple to use and saves on washing up and messy transfer to a liquidiser (though make sure the end of the blender is fully submerged in the soup or you will end up with it everywhere!). For a really fine soup, you can filter through a sieve.
- **Slow cooker** – I make my soups in a slow cooker unless I am in a hurry and have forgotten to prepare something earlier. Don't worry if you haven't got a slow cooker, the recipes include both techniques where applicable.
- **Chunky soups** – some chunky soups may benefit from a thicker stock/sauce. To achieve this, simply remove about a quarter of the soup and purée, and then return it to the soup.
- **Liquid** – you may need to add more water or stock to your soup depending on your personal preference and how you cook the soup. The higher the temperature when the soup is cooked, the more liquid evaporates.
- **Meat and fish** – although there are soup recipes including meat and fish, a lot are vegetarian. You can add meat to a soup to create more of a broth/casserole. When you add meat or fish to a recipe, make sure it is well cooked/reheated (if applicable) before serving.

Chicken, Cumin and Harissa Soup

Slow cooker, casserole dish or saucepan

Olive oil	I teaspoon paprika
I onion, finely chopped	I tin of chickpeas
2–3 cloves of garlic, finely chopped	I tin of chopped tomatoes
½ red pepper, finely chopped	300g cooked chicken
I teaspoon ground cumin	500ml chicken stock
2–3 teaspoons Harissa paste	Freshly chopped coriander

To cook on the hob

- Heat the olive oil in a pan and cook the onion, garlic and red pepper until soft. Add the cumin, Harissa paste and paprika and cook for 1–2 minutes.
- Add the remaining ingredients, including half the chopped coriander, and cook on low/medium heat for 30 minutes.
- To serve, add the remaining coriander and a dollop of natural yoghurt or crème fraiche.

To cook in a slow cooker

- If your slow cooker needs to be preheated, turn it on 15 minutes before using. Refer to your manufacturer's instructions for more information on temperatures for your specific model.
- Add all the ingredients apart from the olive oil (which is not needed) and fresh coriander (which you can add later). Make sure the chicken stock is warm when you add it as this will help to maintain the temperature. Turn your slow cooker to low for 6 hours or high for 4 hours. Add half the fresh coriander 20 minutes before serving.
- To serve, add the remaining coriander and a dollop of natural yoghurt or crème fraiche.

Beef and Barley Soup

I recommend making this in a slow cooker as it is a much nicer way of cooking cheaper cuts of beef, making them lovely and tender.

Slow cooker, casserole dish or saucepan

50g pearl barley

Olive oil for frying

1 onion, diced

250g beef steak, diced

2 sticks of celery, diced

2 carrots, diced

2 leeks, diced

1 litre beef stock

1 teaspoon paprika

1 teaspoon mixed herbs

Seasoning to taste

To cook on the hob

- Rinse the pearl barley.
- Heat a little olive oil in the pan and fry the onion until it starts to soften. Add the beef and brown for 3–4 minutes before adding the vegetables.
- Sweat for 5 minutes before adding the remaining ingredients. Cover and cook for 50 minutes–1 hour on a low heat. Season to taste before serving.

To cook in a slow cooker

- If your slow cooker needs to be preheated, turn it on 15 minutes before using. Refer to your manufacturer's instructions for more information on temperatures for your specific model.
- Rinse the pearl barley.
- Add all the ingredients apart from the olive oil (which is not needed). If you would like to brown the meat beforehand (this is just to achieve the colour), cook in a little olive oil before placing in the slow cooker.
- Make sure the beef stock is warm when you add it as this will maintain the temperature.
- Turn your slow cooker to low for 6 hours or high for 4 hours.
- Season to taste before serving.

Squash Soup with Spiced Yoghurt

This is one of my favourites – the spiced yoghurt really adds to the flavour. It's a perfect autumn soup, making use of the cheap squash on offer.

Slow cooker, casserole dish or saucepan

Olive oil	1–2 teaspoons curry powder (according to taste)
1 onion, diced	1 cooking apple, diced
1–2 cloves of garlic, crushed	500ml water or vegetable stock
1 teaspoon coriander seeds	Seasoning to taste
25g butter	200g natural yoghurt
1 butternut squash	1 chilli, finely chopped
1 teaspoon ground coriander	1 teaspoon hot paprika

To cook on the hob
- Sauté the onions, garlic and coriander seeds in olive oil for 3–4 minutes to help soften.
- Add the butter, butternut squash, ground coriander and curry powder and cook for a further 3–4 minutes.
- Add the apple before adding the stock. Put a lid on the pan and cook on low/medium heat for 30 minutes until the vegetables are tender.
- Season to taste before liquidising. (I use my electric hand/stick blender rather than transferring to a liquidiser – this saves washing up!)
- In a separate bowl, mix the yoghurt, chilli and paprika together.
- To serve, add a dollop of yoghurt mixture in the centre of the soup.

To cook in a slow cooker
- If your slow cooker needs to be preheated, turn it on 15 minutes before using. Refer to your manufacturer's instructions for more information on temperatures for your specific model.
- Add all the ingredients apart from the olive oil (which is not needed).
- Make sure the water or vegetable stock is warm when you add it as this will maintain the temperature. Turn your slow cooker to low for 6 hours or high for 4 hours.
- Season to taste before liquidising. (I use my electric hand/stick blender rather than transferring to a liquidiser – this saves washing up and avoids having to remove the soup from the slow cooker, so is ideal for reheating).
- In a separate bowl, mix the yoghurt, chilli and paprika together.
- To serve, add a dollop of yoghurt mixture in the centre of the soup.

Chicken and Tomato Soup

Slow cooker, casserole dish or saucepan

Olive oil

1 red onion, finely chopped

2 cloves of garlic, crushed

1 red pepper, finely diced

2 sticks of celery, finely diced

1 tin of tomatoes (or 8 ripe tomatoes, finely chopped)

1–2 teaspoons tomato purée (I prefer sun-dried tomato purée)

250g cooked chicken, diced

2 teaspoons paprika

500ml chicken stock

Seasoning to taste

1 bay leaf

To cook on the hob

- Heat the olive oil and add the onion and garlic. Allow to soften before adding the diced pepper and celery. Cook for 2–3 minutes.
- Add the tomatoes and tomato purée before adding the cooked chicken and paprika. Gradually add the chicken stock.
- Season and add the bay leaf. Leave to cook on a low heat for 30 minutes before serving.

To cook in a slow cooker

- If your slow cooker needs to be preheated, turn it on 15 minutes before using. Refer to your manufacturer's instructions for more information on temperatures for your specific model.
- Add all the ingredients apart from the olive oil (which is not needed). Make sure the chicken stock is warm when you add it as this will maintain the temperature. Turn your slow cooker to low for 6 hours or high for 4 hours.
- Season to taste before serving.

Red Pepper and Tomato Soup with Pesto Swirl

Slow cooker, casserole dish or saucepan

Olive oil	4–6 fresh tomatoes, peeled and chopped
1 large onion, chopped	1 teaspoon paprika
1–2 cloves garlic, crushed	900ml–1 litre of water (or home-made stock)
4 red peppers deseeded and chopped	Black pepper to taste
½ teaspoon mild chilli powder	Pesto (fresh or jar)

To cook on the hob

- Heat the oil and cook the onion, garlic and peppers together in a pan until soft and the onions are translucent. Add the chilli powder and stir well.
- Add the tomatoes and cook for 2 minutes. Add the paprika and water. Season to taste. Cook slowly on a low heat for 1 hour.
- Cool slightly. Use an electric hand blender to purée. Reheat when ready to serve.
- Pour the soup into bowls and add a spoonful of pesto to the centre of each bowl. Using a sharp knife, swirl the pesto from the centre of the bowls.

To cook in a slow cooker

- If your slow cooker needs to be preheated, turn it on 15 minutes before using. Refer to your manufacturer's instructions for more information on temperatures for your specific model.
- Add all the ingredients apart from the olive oil (which is not needed). Make sure the water is warm when you add it as this will maintain the temperature. Turn your slow cooker to low for 6 hours.
- Use an electric hand blender to purée. Reheat when ready to serve.
- Place the soup in a bowl and add a spoonful of pesto to the centre. Using a sharp knife, swirl the pesto from the centre of the bowl.

Gammon and Parsnip Soup

This is a great recipe for using up any leftover gammon joint and vegetables.

Slow cooker, casserole dish or saucepan

25g butter	1 bay leaf
1 onion, finely chopped	A small handful of freshly chopped parsley
2 cloves of garlic, crushed	Seasoning to taste
1 carrot, diced	200g *cooked* gammon, cut into chunks
2–3 parsnips, diced	Single cream
1 litre of vegetable stock	

To cook on the hob

- Melt the butter in your stock pan. Add the onion, garlic, carrot and parsnips and allow to sweat for 5–6 minutes.
- Pour over the stock, add the bay leaf and parsley and season to taste. Cook on medium heat for 20–30 minutes.
- Remove from heat and remove the bay leaf. Purée gently (I use the electric hand/stick blender). You can leave some chunkiness to the soup, just purée enough to form a creamy consistency.
- Add the gammon pieces and return to a low heat and cook for 20 minutes (you can transfer to a slow cooker if you prefer).
- To serve, place the soup in bowls and add a swirl of single cream to each bowl.

To cook in a slow cooker

- If your slow cooker needs to be preheated, turn it on 15 minutes before using. Refer to your manufacturer's instructions for more information on temperatures for your specific model.
- Add all the ingredients apart from the butter (which you don't need), the gammon and the cream (which will be added later).
- Make sure the stock is warm when you add it as this will maintain the temperature. Turn your slow cooker to low for 6 hours.
- Liquidise with your electric hand/stick blender. Add the cooked gammon chunks and turn onto high and cook for 30–45 minutes.
- Season to taste and serve with a swirl of cream in the centre of each bowl.

Note: If you prefer, you can add the gammon when you add the stock and cook in one batch, before puréeing. I prefer to do this the other way as I think the gammon chunks look more attractive in the creamy soup, but it is personal preference.

Carrot, Tomato and Basil Soup

Slow cooker, casserole dish or saucepan

Olive oil

1 onion

1–2 cloves of garlic, crushed

30g fresh basil leaves

1–2 carrots, diced

400g tomatoes (you can use tinned if you prefer, but fresh tastes best!)

1–2 teaspoons of sun-dried tomato purée

500ml water or stock

½ teaspoon oregano

Seasoning to taste

To cook on the hob

• Heat the olive oil in a pan and cook the onion and garlic for 3–4 minutes to help soften.

• Add half the fresh basil and all the remaining ingredients, and cook on a low to medium heat for 20 minutes.

• Add the remaining basil and cook for a further 5–10 minutes.

• Season to taste before serving.

To cook in a slow cooker

• If your slow cooker needs to be preheated, turn it on 15 minutes before using. Refer to your manufacturer's instructions for more information on temperatures for your specific model.

• Add all the ingredients apart from the olive oil (which is not needed). Make sure the water or stock is warm when you add it as this will maintain the temperature. Turn your slow cooker to low for 6 hours.

• Season to taste before serving.

Mint and Green Pea Soup

Casserole dish or saucepan

1 teaspoon olive oil or a knob of butter

4–6 spring onions, chopped to include most of the green stalks

400g fresh peas (you can use frozen if not in season)

500ml water

A small handful of fresh pea pods, chopped finely (ignore this if you are using frozen peas)

2–3 sprigs of fresh mint

Black pepper to season

A swirl of low fat crème fraiche and a sprig of fresh mint to garnish

- Heat the butter or oil in a pan and cook the spring onions for 2 minutes. Add the pea pods and cook for a further 2 minutes.
- Add the water, peas and mint, season with black pepper and cook gently on a low heat for 45 minutes–1 hour.
- Cool slightly. Use an electric hand blender to purée the soup and return it to the pan until you are ready to serve. Alternatively, you can place it in the fridge to serve chilled.
- Add a dollop of low fat crème fraiche to each bowl and swirl from the centre. Garnish with a sprig of fresh mint.

Spicy Vegetable and Lentil Soup

This is a great winter warmer and ideal for using up any spare vegetables lurking in the bottom of your fridge. You can adjust the spices to suit your own palate.

Slow cooker or saucepan

Olive oil	2 sticks of celery, sliced
1 onion, finely chopped	1–2 sweet potatoes, diced
2–3 cloves of garlic, crushed	2 carrots, diced
½ a chilli, finely chopped	3 tomatoes, finely chopped
2.5cm (1in) knuckle of ginger, finely chopped	125g red lentils
1 teaspoon cumin seeds	400ml passata or tomato juice
1 teaspoon cumin	1 litre vegetable stock
1 teaspoon garam masala	Seasoning to taste
½ teaspoon of turmeric	

To cook on the hob

- Place the oil, onion, garlic, chilli and ginger in a saucepan and heat gently until the onion starts to soften. Add the spices and cook for another 2–3 minutes to release the flavours.
- Add the vegetables and allow to sweat for 5 minutes before adding the lentils, passata/tomato juice, vegetable stock and seasoning.
- Cover and cook slowly on a medium heat for 30–45 minutes, until the vegetables are tender.

To cook in a slow cooker

- Sauté the onions, garlic, chilli and ginger in the oil until the onion starts to soften. (If your slow cooker has a sauté facility or can be removed and used directly on the hob, do this. Alternatively, you can prepare the first stage in a frying/sauté pan then transfer to the slow cooker.)
- Add the spices and cook gently for 2–3 minutes to release the flavours. Transfer to the preheated slow cooker (refer to your manufacturer's guidelines on temperatures).
- Add all the remaining ingredients. Turn your slow cooker to high and cook for 6–8 hours.
- You can purée the soup if you want a smooth soup, or you can remove a small amount of soup, purée and return to the pan – this gives a thicker base but retains the chunkiness of the vegetables. Season and serve with crusty bread, naan or pitta bread.

Avocado Soup

Use up your ripe avocados in this recipe. Serve hot or cold.

Liquidiser or saucepan

3 ripe avocados	750ml hot chicken or vegetable stock
Juice and zest of 1 lemon	200g low fat crème fraiche
1–2 cloves of garlic, crushed	Coriander leaves
1 chilli, chopped finely	Seasoning to taste

- Place the avocados, lemon, garlic and chilli in a liquidiser and blend until smooth.
- Add the hot stock, crème fraiche and coriander leaves and whizz again. Season to taste.
- Serve hot or cold.

Cream-free Broccoli and Stilton Soup

This recipe avoids the traditional use of cream and milk, so is lower in fat than most recipes. However, you can add cream if you prefer the taste.

Casserole dish or saucepan

1 teaspoon olive oil	2–3 heads of broccoli
1 onion, chopped	900ml water, stock or milk
1 small leek, finely chopped	120g Stilton cheese, crumbled
2 cooked potatoes, chopped	Black pepper to taste

- Heat the oil in a pan and cook the onions and leeks until soft and translucent.
- Add the potatoes, broccoli and water or stock and cook for 30 minutes on a low heat until tender.
- Cool slightly. Use an electric hand blender to purée and return the soup to the pan until you are ready to serve.
- Add the cheese and cook for a couple of minutes prior to serving, until the cheese melts.
- Season to taste.

Note: If you prefer the soup with a creamier flavour, add a few spoonfuls of low fat crème fraiche when you add the Stilton.

Cream of Celeriac Soup

Slow cooker, casserole dish or saucepan

Olive oil	750g celeriac, sliced
1 onion	1 white potato, diced
2 cloves of garlic, crushed	750ml vegetable stock
1–2 leeks, sliced	1 bay leaf
25g butter	250ml milk
1 stick of celery, sliced	2 tablespoons low fat crème fraiche
1 green pepper, diced	Seasoning to taste

To cook on the hob
- Sauté the onion, garlic and leeks in olive oil for 4–5 minutes.
- Add butter, celery, pepper, celeriac and potato and allow to sweat in the pan for a further 5 minutes.
- Add the vegetable stock, bay leaf and milk and cover. Leave to cook on a low/medium heat for 30–45 minutes.
- Liquidise and then add crème fraiche and season to taste. Reheat gently before serving.

To cook in a slow cooker
- If your slow cooker needs to be preheated, turn it on 15 minutes before using. Refer to your manufacturer's instructions for more information on temperatures for your specific model.
- Add all the ingredients apart from the olive oil (which is not needed). Make sure the stock is warm when you add it as this will maintain the temperature. Turn your slow cooker to low for 6 hours.
- Use your electric hand/stick blender and liquidise the soup until smooth. Add the crème fraiche and season to taste. Reheat gently before serving.

Tomato Soup

Tomato soup never fails to cheer me up – it's like a hug in a bowl or mug. For an extra treat, enjoy with some cheese on toast – delicious!

Slow cooker, casserole dish or saucepan

1 teaspoon olive oil	50g sun-dried tomatoes
1 onion, finely chopped	½ stick of celery, finely chopped
1 clove garlic, crushed	450ml water
800g fresh tomatoes, peeled and finely chopped	1 teaspoon paprika
2 teaspoons sun-dried tomato purée	Black pepper to taste

To cook on the hob

- Heat the oil in a pan and fry the onion and garlic until translucent.
- Add all the remaining ingredients to the pan and leave to cook slowly on a low heat for 45 minutes–1 hour.
- Cool slightly. Use an electric hand blender to purée and return the soup to the pan until you are ready to serve.
- Garnish with basil leaves.

To cook in a slow cooker

- If your slow cooker needs to be preheated, turn it on 15 minutes before using. Refer to your manufacturer's instructions for more information on temperatures for your specific model.
- Add all the ingredients apart from the olive oil (which is not needed). Make sure the stock is warm when you add it as this will maintain the temperature. Turn your slow cooker to low for 6 hours.
- Use your electric hand/stick blender and liquidise the soup until smooth. Reheat gently before serving.

Minestrone Soup

Slow cooker, casserole dish or saucepan

1 teaspoon olive oil	500ml water or fresh stock
1 large onion, chopped	3 teaspoons pure tomato purée
1 clove garlic, crushed	½ teaspoon cayenne pepper
1 red pepper, finely chopped	1 teaspoon paprika
1 carrot, diced	2 bay leaves
½ celery stick, finely chopped	50g cabbage, shredded
3–4 fresh tomatoes, peeled and chopped	40g dried spaghetti
50g red kidney beans, cooked	1 tablespoon fresh basil
50g fresh green beans, chopped	Seasoning to taste

To cook on the hob

- Heat the oil in the base of your casserole dish or heavy saucepan and cook the onion and garlic until translucent and soft. Add the pepper and cook for another 2 minutes.
- Place all the remaining ingredients except the cabbage, basil and spaghetti into the pan and cook slowly on a low heat for 45 minutes–1 hour.
- Twenty minutes before serving add the shredded cabbage, dried spaghetti (broken into smaller pieces) and basil.
- Serve with crusty bread and hummus for a hearty meal.

To cook in a slow cooker

- If your slow cooker needs to be preheated, turn it on 15 minutes before using. Refer to your manufacturer's instructions for more information on temperatures for your specific model.
- Add all the ingredients apart from the olive oil (which is not needed), cabbage, spaghetti, cayenne and basil. Make sure the stock is warm when you add it as this will maintain the temperature. Turn your slow cooker to low for 6 hours.
- About 30–45 minutes before serving, add the cabbage, dried spaghetti (broken into smaller pieces), cayenne and basil. Turn slow cooker up to high.
- Serve with crusty bread and hummus.

Note: Be aware that red kidney beans *must* be precooked thoroughly before you add them to the slow cooker! Tinned are safe to add straight from the can. Red kidney beans that are not cooked correctly could cause food poisoning.

Rich Vegetable Soup

This also makes a lovely casserole if you leave the vegetables chunky.

Slow cooker, casserole dish or saucepan

1 teaspoon olive oil	500ml stock or water
1 medium onion, coarsely chopped	100ml apple juice
1–2 cloves garlic, crushed	2 teaspoons paprika
¼ swede, finely chopped	A dash of cayenne pepper
1 parsnip, finely chopped	2 bay leaves
3 medium tomatoes, chopped	½ teaspoon dill
2 small carrots, chopped	Seasoning to taste
1 small celery stalk with leaves, chopped	2 teaspoons of chopped parsley to garnish
1 small apple, chopped	

To cook on the hob

- Heat the oil in the base of your saucepan or casserole dish and cook the onion and garlic until translucent and soft.
- Place all the remaining ingredients (except the herbs) into your pan and cook on a low heat for 1–1½ hours.
- Add the herbs 20 minutes before serving. If you want a smooth soup, cool slightly. Use an electric hand blender to purée and reheat when you are ready to serve. Alternatively, leave chunky.
- Serve garnished with chopped parsley.

To cook in a slow cooker

- If your slow cooker needs to be preheated, turn it on 15 minutes before using. Refer to your manufacturer's instructions for more information on temperatures for your specific model.
- Add all the ingredients apart from the olive oil (which is not needed). Make sure the stock is warm when you add it as this will maintain the temperature. Turn your slow cooker to low for 6–8 hours.
- If you prefer a smooth soup, you can use your electric hand/stick blender and liquidise until smooth. Reheat gently before serving and garnish with chopped parsley.

Cream of Split Pea Soup

Slow cooker, casserole dish or saucepan

100g yellow split peas	1 teaspoon caraway seeds
1 teaspoon olive oil	¼ teaspoon of ground mace
1 medium onion, chopped	1 bay leaf
1–2 cloves of garlic, crushed	750–900ml of water or stock
1 large potato, diced	Seasoning to taste
1 stick of celery	

To cook on the hob
- Steep the split peas in hot water for an hour and drain.
- Heat the oil in the base of a casserole dish or heavy saucepan and cook the onion and garlic until translucent and soft.
- Add all the remaining ingredients and cook for 1 hour on a low heat.
- Cool slightly and remove the bay leaf. Use an electric hand blender to purée the soup and reheat when you are ready to serve.

To cook in a slow cooker
- If your slow cooker needs to be preheated, turn it on 15 minutes before using. Refer to your manufacturer's instructions for more information on temperatures for your specific model.
- Add all the ingredients apart from the olive oil (which is not needed). Make sure the stock is warm when you add it as this will maintain the temperature. Turn your slow cooker to low for 6–8 hours.
- Remove the bay leaf. Use your electric hand/stick blender and liquidise until smooth. Serve immediately or reheat gently before serving.

Chilli, Prawn and Noodle Soup

I have shamelessly pinched this recipe from a friend of mine who discovered the original online and has since adapted it. It is a big hit with her family and friends, so I hope you enjoy it too.

Sauté pan or saucepan

Olive oil

1 bunch of spring onions, finely chopped

2–3 cloves of garlic, crushed

2.5–5cm (1–2in) knuckle of ginger, finely chopped

1 chilli, finely chopped

200g tiger prawns, shelled

75g creamed coconut

400ml water

500ml fish stock

4–6 teaspoons fish sauce

100g fresh rice noodles

A handful of fresh coriander

- Heat the oil in the saucepan/sauté pan, add the spring onions, garlic, ginger and chilli and cook for 2 minutes to release the flavours.
- Add the prawns and cook for 1–2 minutes before adding the coconut, water and fish stock. Cook for 5 minutes before adding the remaining ingredients.
- Cook for a further 5 minutes before serving.

Carrot and Coriander Soup

Slow cooker, casserole dish or saucepan

1 teaspoon olive oil

2 teaspoons ground coriander

1 teaspoon ground cumin

1 onion, chopped

1 clove garlic

3 carrots, diced

2 celery sticks, finely chopped

500ml water or stock

Seasoning to taste

1 teaspoon finely chopped coriander leaves
  (optional)

To cook on the hob

- Heat the oil in the base of a heavy saucepan or casserole dish. Add the spices and cook for no more than 1 minute.
- Add all the remaining ingredients and leave to cook on a low heat for 1 hour.
- Cool slightly. Use an electric hand blender to purée the soup and reheat when you are ready to serve.
- Season and garnish with chopped coriander leaves. Serve hot.

To cook in a slow cooker

- If your slow cooker needs to be preheated, turn it on 15 minutes before using. Refer to your manufacturer's instructions for more information on temperatures for your specific model.
- Add all the ingredients apart from the olive oil (which is not needed). Make sure the stock is warm when you add it as this will maintain the temperature. Turn your slow cooker to low for 6–8 hours.
- Use your electric hand/stick blender and liquidise until smooth. Reheat gently before serving.

Country Vegetable Broth

Anything goes with this soup! It is excellent for using up vegetables that are nearing their use by date.

Slow cooker, casserole dish or saucepan

Olive oil	1 carrot, diced
1 onion, chopped	700–900ml vegetable stock or water
1 clove of garlic	2 teaspoons tomato purée (optional)
25g green split peas	1–2 bay leaves
25g red lentils	1–2 teaspoons paprika
1 medium parsnip, diced	2 teaspoons rosemary, freshly chopped
1 sweet potato, diced	1 teaspoon thyme, finely chopped
1 medium potato, diced	Seasoning to taste

To cook on the hob
- Heat the oil in the base of a casserole dish or heavy saucepan and cook the onion and garlic until translucent and soft.
- Add all the remaining ingredients (except the herbs) to the pan and leave to cook on a low heat for 1–1½ hours.
- Stir in the herbs and season to taste. You can serve the soup immediately, just as it is, or blend it briefly in a liquidiser or with a hand blender for a smoother texture. Do not liquidise it completely or it will lose its character.

To cook in a slow cooker
- If your slow cooker needs to be preheated, turn it on 15 minutes before using. Refer to your manufacturer's instructions for more information on temperatures for your specific model.
- Add all the ingredients apart from the olive oil (which is not needed). Make sure the stock is warm when you add it as this will maintain the temperature. Turn your slow cooker to low for 6–8 hours.
- You can liquidise slightly if you prefer a half smooth, half chunky soup. Reheat gently before serving.

Note: You can substitute 50g of dried soup mix (containing a range of pulses and barley) for the lentils and split peas.

Roasted Pumpkin Soup

This makes a delicious warming dish for Halloween or you can use other squash for an all-year treat.

Ovenproof dish and saucepan

Olive oil

1 small pumpkin

1 onion

1 garlic clove, crushed

1 teaspoon grated root ginger

1 teaspoon grated nutmeg

½ teaspoon ground coriander

1–2 carrots, chopped

1 medium sweet potato

2 sticks of celery

4 tomatoes, peeled and chopped

2 teaspoons of tomato purée (optional)

300–425ml water or stock

15ml lemon juice

Seasoning to taste

- Cut the pumpkin into wedges, coat with a light brush of oil and place in the oven on a low heat (160°C/gas mark 3) for 20 minutes.
- Meanwhile prepare the vegetables. Cook the onion, garlic and spices together in a saucepan until soft and the onions are translucent.
- Take the flesh from the pumpkin wedges and place with the spices. Add all the other ingredients.
- Cook slowly on a low heat for 1 hour. Cool slightly. Use an electric hand blender to purée and return to the pan until you are ready to serve.
- Season as required.
- For impressive presentation, use hollowed pumpkins as serving dishes.

Carrot, Tomato and Lentil Soup

This is a really tasty and wholesome soup that kids and adults adore. As with most of the soups in this chapter, you can cook it on the hob or in the slow cooker.

Slow cooker, casserole dish or saucepan

Olive oil	1 teaspoon dried basil *or* a bunch of fresh basil,
1 large onion	chopped
1–2 cloves garlic	570ml water or stock
2 teaspoons paprika	125g lentils, washed
6–8 tomatoes chopped	2 dessertspoons tomato purée (optional)
2 carrots, chopped	½ red pepper
	1 bay leaf

To cook on the hob

- Heat the oil in a casserole dish or saucepan and cook the onion, garlic and paprika together until soft and the onions are translucent. Chop all the remaining vegetables and add to the pan with the herbs, lentils, tomato purée and bay leaf.
- Cover with water or stock. Cook slowly on a low heat for 1 hour.
- Cool slightly. Use an electric hand blender to purée and reheat when you are ready to serve.

To cook in a slow cooker

- If your slow cooker needs to be preheated, turn it on 15 minutes before using. Refer to your manufacturer's instructions for more information on temperatures for your specific model.
- Add all the ingredients apart from the olive oil (which is not needed). Make sure the stock is warm when you add it as this will maintain the temperature. Turn your slow cooker to low for 6–8 hours.
- Use your electric hand/stick blender and liquidise until smooth. Reheat gently before serving.

Butter Bean and Vegetable Soup

Slow cooker, casserole dish or saucepan

225g butter beans	2 carrots, chopped
500–900ml water or stock	1 parsnip, chopped
25g butter	½ teaspoon dried thyme
2 leeks, finely sliced	Black pepper to taste

To cook on the hob
- If using dried butter beans, soak the butter beans overnight in lots of water.
- Rinse the beans well and cook in the stock or water until soft, adding more water if the liquid is evaporating. When cooked, place to one side. Alternatively, you can use canned butter beans.
- Heat the butter in a saucepan and cook the leeks until soft. Add the remaining vegetables and cook for a further 2 minutes before adding all the remaining ingredients.
- Place on a low heat and cook slowly for 1 hour.
- Season to taste before serving.

To cook in a slow cooker
- If your slow cooker needs to be preheated, turn it on 15 minutes before using. Refer to your manufacturer's instructions for more information on temperatures for your specific model.
- I would suggest you use tinned butter beans for this. Add all the ingredients apart from the butter (which is not needed). Make sure the stock is warm when you add it as this will maintain the temperature. Turn your slow cooker to low for 6–8 hours.
- Season to taste before serving.

Carrot and Courgette Soup

Slow cooker, casserole dish or saucepan

Olive oil	1–2 teaspoons grated fresh ginger
1 onion, chopped	900ml water or stock
2–3 carrots, diced	1 teaspoon dried or fresh thyme
1 sweet potato, diced	2–3 courgettes, diced

To cook on the hob
- Heat a dash of olive oil in a saucepan and cook the onion until soft and translucent.
- Add the carrots and sweet potato and cook for a further couple of minutes to help soften. Add the fresh ginger and cook for another minute.
- Add all the remaining ingredients. Cook slowly on a low heat for 45 minutes– 1 hour.
- You can leave the soup as is or, if you want a smooth soup, cool slightly. Use an electric hand blender to purée and return to the pan until you are ready to serve.

To cook in a slow cooker
- If your slow cooker needs to be preheated, turn it on 15 minutes before using. Refer to your manufacturer's instructions for more information on temperatures for your specific model.
- Add all the ingredients apart from the olive oil (which is not needed). Make sure the stock is warm when you add it as this will maintain the temperature. Turn your slow cooker to low for 6–8 hours.
- Use your electric hand/stick blender and liquidise until smooth. Reheat gently before serving.

Mulligatawny Soup

Slow cooker, casserole dish or saucepan

Olive oil	1 litre water or stock
1 large onion, chopped	Seasoning to taste
1–2 cloves garlic	2 bay leaves
1 tablespoon garam masala or curry powder	1 tablespoon lemon juice
2–3 carrots, diced	75g long-grain rice
1 sweet potato, diced	1 chicken breast fillet, cubed
1 parsnip, diced	(vegetarians can omit)
1 cooking apple	Fresh coriander leaves or parsley to garnish

To cook on the hob

- Heat the olive oil and cook the onion, garlic and spices together in a saucepan until soft and the onions are translucent. Add the carrot, sweet potato, parsnip and apple and sweat together for 5 minutes.
- Add the water or stock, seasoning and bay leaves. Cover and cook for 15 minutes on medium heat.
- Add the lemon juice and check the seasoning, adding a little more garam masala if required.
- Add the rice and the chicken, if using. Cover and cook for a further 15–20 minutes.
- Garnish with chopped coriander leaves or parsley.

To cook in a slow cooker

- If your slow cooker needs to be preheated, turn it on 15 minutes before using. Refer to your manufacturer's instructions for more information on temperatures for your specific model.
- Add all the ingredients apart from the olive oil (which is not needed). Make sure the stock is warm when you add it as this will maintain the temperature. Turn your slow cooker to low for 6–8 hours.
- Garnish with some fresh herbs before serving.

Nettle Soup

It sounds scary but nettles make a wonderful tasty soup. Make sure you wear gloves when you are collecting them. Choose the newest stems and wash before use.

Slow cooker, casserole dish or saucepan

500g young organic nettles (wear gloves when picking!)	1 potato, diced
25g butter or olive oil	1 leek, chopped
1 large onion	900ml water
2 cloves of garlic, crushed	Black pepper to taste
	2–3 tablespoons low fat crème fraiche

To cook on the hob
- Thoroughly wash and chop the nettles (you may want to wear gloves for this).
- Heat the butter or oil in a pan and fry the onion and garlic until soft. Add the potato and leek and cook for a further 5 minutes.
- Add the water and nettles to the pan and season with black pepper. Cook slowly on a low heat for 45 minutes–1 hour.
- Cool slightly. Use an electric hand blender to purée the soup and reheat when you are ready to serve.
- Add the crème fraiche. Check the seasoning and serve the soup garnished with chopped fresh sage or parsley.

To cook in a slow cooker
- If your slow cooker needs to be preheated, turn it on 15 minutes before using. Refer to your manufacturer's instructions for more information on temperatures for your specific model.
- Add all the ingredients apart from the butter or olive oil (which is not needed). Make sure the stock is warm when you add it as this will maintain the temperature. Turn your slow cooker to low for 6 hours.
- Use your electric hand/stick blender and liquidise until smooth. Add the crème fraiche and season to taste. Reheat gently before serving.

Variation
For a change, you can use the green tops of red radishes instead of nettles.

Watercress Soup

Saucepan

25g butter	150–200g watercress
1 onion, chopped	300ml semi-skimmed milk
2 potatoes, chopped	Seasoning to taste
600ml water or stock	

- Heat the butter in a saucepan and cook the onion until soft and translucent. Add the potatoes and cook for a further 5 minutes.
- Add the water or stock and watercress. Cook slowly on a low heat for 30–45 minutes, until the potatoes are tender.
- Cool slightly. Use an electric hand blender to purée and return the soup to the pan. Add the milk and season to taste.
- Reheat gently when you are ready to serve.

Sweet Potato, Carrot and Parsnip Soup

Slow cooker, casserole dish or saucepan

25g butter

1 leek, sliced

2 celery sticks, chopped

3–4 sweet potatoes, cubed

2–3 carrots, cubed

1 parsnip, cubed

1 litre water or stock

15ml fresh chopped parsley

Fresh ground black pepper to taste

To cook on the hob

- Heat the butter in a large saucepan and fry the leek until soft. Place all the remaining vegetables into the pan and sweat for another 5 minutes.
- Add the water or stock, and the parsley. Cook slowly on a low heat for 45 minutes or until the vegetables are tender.
- Season to taste with black pepper.
- If you want to thicken the soup, remove about a quarter of the cooled soup and liquid, and liquidise until smooth. Return the liquidised soup to the pan and reheat gently before serving.
- Serve sprinkled with parsley garnish.

To cook in a slow cooker

- If your slow cooker needs to be preheated, turn it on 15 minutes before using. Refer to your manufacturer's instructions for more information on temperatures for your specific model.
- Add all the ingredients apart from the butter (which is not needed). Make sure the stock is warm when you add it as this will maintain the temperature. Turn your slow cooker to low for 6–8 hours.
- If you like a smooth soup, you can use your electric hand/stick blender to liquidise until smooth. Reheat gently before serving.
- Serve sprinkled with parsley garnish.

Tuna and Sweetcorn Chowder

This is a really simple soup that takes minutes to make.

Saucepan

Olive oil	I can of tuna, drained
I onion, finely chopped	I can of sweetcorn, drained
2 cloves of garlic, crushed	I bay leaf
2 sticks of celery, finely chopped	A handful of fresh thyme
I tablespoon plain flour or cornflour	A handful of fresh parsley
I litre milk	Seasoning to taste

- Heat the oil in a pan and fry the onion, garlic and celery until the onion starts to soften.
- Add the flour and stir well, absorbing all the juices. Gradually add the milk and keep stirring until the mixture starts to thicken.
- Add the tuna, sweetcorn, bay leaf, thyme and parsley. Bring to simmering point and cook for 5–8 minutes. Season to taste.
- Remove the bay leaf and serve.

Leek and Potato Soup

This is a family favourite in our house. I hope you also enjoy it.

Slow cooker, casserole dish or saucepan

25g butter	4 tablespoons low fat crème fraiche
2–3 leeks, sliced or chopped	½ tablespoon parsley
2 potatoes, cubed	1 tablespoon fresh sage
700ml water/stock	Black pepper to taste
300ml semi-skimmed milk	1 teaspoon chives

To cook on the hob
- Heat the butter in a saucepan and cook the leeks until soft. Add the potato and cook for a further 5 minutes.
- Cover with water or stock. Cook slowly on a low heat for 30–45 minutes. Add the milk, crème fraiche, parsley and sage and cook for a further 5 minutes. Season to taste.
- Cool slightly. Use an electric hand blender to purée the soup and return to the pan until you are ready to serve.
- Garnish with chopped chives

To cook in a slow cooker
- If your slow cooker needs to be preheated, turn it on 15 minutes before using. Refer to your manufacturer's instructions for more information on temperatures for your specific model.
- Add all the ingredients apart from the butter (which is not needed), milk and crème fraiche. Make sure the water or stock is warm when you add it as this will maintain the temperature. Turn your slow cooker to low for 6–8 hours.
- Use your electric hand/stick blender and liquidise until smooth. Add the milk and crème fraiche and season to taste. Reheat gently before serving.

Sweet Potato and Butternut Squash Soup

I love sweet potatoes – they are such a vibrant colour and packed full of goodness.

Slow cooker, casserole dish or saucepan

Olive oil

1 onion, chopped

1–2 cloves garlic, crushed

1 teaspoon coriander seeds

1–2 teaspoons freshly grated ginger

2 sweet potatoes, diced

1 stick of celery, diced

1 small carrot, diced

½ small butternut squash, peeled and cubed

1 litre water or stock

Seasoning to taste

To cook on the hob

- Heat the oil in a saucepan and cook the onion, garlic and coriander seeds together until soft and the onions are translucent. Add the grated ginger and cook for a further minute.
- Add the potatoes, celery, carrot and squash and a little of the water/stock and cook for another 5 minutes to help soften.
- Add all the remaining water/stock. Cook slowly on a low heat for 45 minutes.
- Cool slightly. Use an electric hand blender to purée the soup and return to the pan until you are ready to serve.
- Season to taste before serving.

To cook in a slow cooker

- If your slow cooker needs to be preheated, turn it on 15 minutes before using. Refer to your manufacturer's instructions for more information on temperatures for your specific model.
- Add all the ingredients apart from the olive oil (which is not needed). Make sure the stock is warm when you add it as this will maintain the temperature. Turn your slow cooker to low for 6 hours.
- Use your electric hand/stick blender and liquidise the soup until smooth. Reheat gently before serving.

Note: Serve with a swirl of chilli sauce for added zing.

Scotch Broth

Slow cooker, casserole dish or saucepan

Olive oil	75g soup mix
1 onion, diced	¼ small cabbage
1 leek, finely chopped	1 litre water or stock
1 carrot, cubed	1 bay leaf
1 parsnip, cubed	Seasoning to taste
400g beef skirt, sliced thinly	

To cook on the hob

- Heat the oil in a saucepan and cook the onion and leek together until soft and the onion is translucent.
- Add the carrot and parsnip and cook for a further 5 minutes.
- Add the beef skirt slices and brown for 2–4 minutes before adding all the remaining ingredients.
- Cook slowly on a low heat for 45 minutes–1 hour.
- Season to taste before serving.

To cook in a slow cooker

- If your slow cooker needs to be preheated, turn it on 15 minutes before using. Refer to your manufacturer's instructions for more information on temperatures for your specific model.
- If you would like to brown the meat beforehand (this is just to achieve the colour), fry in a little olive oil before placing in the slow cooker. Add all the remaining ingredients to the slow cooker.
- Make sure the beef stock is warm when you add it as this will maintain the temperature. Turn your slow cooker to low for 6–8 hours or high for 4–6 hours.
- Season to taste before serving.

Sweet Potato, Apple and Ginger Soup

Slow cooker, casserole dish or saucepan

Olive oil	2–3 teaspoons grated fresh ginger
1 onion	(depending on desired strength)
2 sweet potatoes, chopped	700ml water or stock
2 sticks of celery, chopped	30ml lemon juice
2 cooking apples, chopped	Seasoning to taste
	Coriander leaves to garnish

To cook on the hob

- Heat the oil in a saucepan and cook the onion until translucent. Add the sweet potatoes, celery and apples and sweat for another 5 minutes.
- Add the grated ginger and cook for 2 more minutes. Add a dash of water if the mixture is too dry.
- Add the water/stock, cover the pan with a lid and cook slowly on a low heat for 45 minutes.
- Cool slightly. Use an electric hand blender to purée. Add lemon juice and seasoning to taste.
- Reheat the soup gently before serving. Garnish with coriander leaves.

To cook in a slow cooker

- If your slow cooker needs to be preheated, turn it on 15 minutes before using. Refer to your manufacturer's instructions for more information on temperatures for your specific model.
- Add all the ingredients apart from the olive oil (which is not needed), lemon juice and coriander leaves. Make sure the water/stock is warm when you add it as this will maintain the temperature. Turn your slow cooker to low for 6–8 hours.
- Use your electric hand/stick blender and liquidise the soup until smooth. Season and add lemon juice to taste. Reheat gently before serving. Garnish with coriander leaves.

Pea Soup

Saucepan

25g butter
1 onion, finely chopped
1–2 cloves garlic, crushed
1 medium potato, diced
700ml water or stock

400g peas (fresh peas give a richer taste)
2 tablespoons fresh chopped mint
Seasoning to taste
Crème fraiche

- Melt the butter in a pan and fry the onion and garlic for 2 minutes.
- Add the potato and cook for a further 3–4 minutes.
- Add the water or stock and cook for 10 minutes, or until the potato is tender.
- Add the peas and mint, and cook for a further 10 minutes.
- Cool slightly. Use an electric hand blender to purée the soup and return it to the pan. Add seasoning to taste and 1 large spoonful of crème fraiche. Stir well and reheat gently.
- Serve warm with a spoonful of crème fraiche and mint leaves to garnish.

Sweetcorn and Haddock Chowder

Saucepan

25g butter

1 onion

2 potatoes, cubed

2 sticks of celery, chopped

2–3 lean smoked bacon rashers, chopped (optional)

500ml water or stock

2 smoked haddock fillets, chopped

200ml semi-skimmed milk

Seasoning to taste

2 teaspoons chopped parsley

- Melt the butter in a large saucepan and fry the onion until translucent.
- Add the potatoes and sweat for 5 minutes. Add the celery and bacon (if using) and cook for another 2 minutes.
- Add half the water/stock and cook for 5 more minutes to help soften the potatoes slightly.
- Add the rest of the water/stock and all the remaining ingredients and cook for 10 minutes.
- Test the haddock to see if it is cooked – it should flake if pressed with a knife or fork.
- Reheat the soup gently. Season to taste. Serve and sprinkle with parsley to garnish.

Chinese-style Beef Broth

Saucepan

Olive oil	4–5 button mushrooms, finely sliced
1 onion	30g bean sprouts
1–2 cloves garlic, crushed	100ml dry sherry
200g thinly sliced beef steak	750ml water or stock
½ red pepper, sliced	1–2 teaspoons soy sauce
5cm (2in) knuckle of ginger, chopped	100g fine noodles
1–2 red chillies	

- Heat the olive oil in a saucepan or casserole dish and sauté the onion and garlic for 2–3 minutes. Add the beef, pepper, ginger and chillies and cook until the beef is brown.
- Add the mushrooms, bean sprouts and sherry. Cook for 2 minutes before adding the stock, soy sauce and noodles.
- Cook for 15 minutes before serving.

One Pot Chicken

Chicken is versatile, cheap and popular with most children – so what could be better for family meals? Here you will find a varied selection of recipes using the one pot or slow cook method.

Salsatouille Chicken

This is a really simple dish, roasted in the oven. If you are not a fan of spices, you could remove the salsa ingredients and just stick with the basic ratatouille mixture.

Roasting tin

Olive oil

2 red onions cut into wedges

1–2 chillies (depending on strength required), finely diced

3–4 garlic cloves, finely sliced

1–2 red peppers, deseeded and thickly sliced

1–2 courgettes, thickly sliced

1 aubergine, sliced

6–8 cherry tomatoes

4 chicken breasts

Sprigs of rosemary and thyme

Paprika

Seasoning to taste

- Preheat your oven to 200°C/gas mark 6.
- Drizzle a generous amount of olive oil into your roasting tin. Add all the vegetables and toss until they are evenly coated.
- Rub some oil into the chicken and finish with a sprinkle of paprika. Place the chicken in the roasting pan with the vegetables. Add the herbs.
- Make sure everything is evenly distributed and the herbs are randomly placed among the vegetables.
- Season well and sprinkle with oil and paprika if needed.
- Place in the oven for 35–40 minutes. Serve in the roasting tin.

Pot Roast Chicken

Roasting tin

1 whole chicken	2 carrots, roughly chopped
30g butter	2 parsnips, roughly chopped
Seasoning	1–2 red peppers, quartered
1 red onion, whole	2–3 teaspoons paprika
1kg new potatoes	Fresh thyme
2 red onions, quartered	Fresh rosemary
2–3 cloves of garlic, roughly chopped	Olive oil

- Preheat the oven to 180°C/gas mark 4.
- Wash and clean the chicken. Rub butter on the chicken skin and season. Insert the whole onion in the chicken cavity. Place the chicken on a large greased/oiled roasting tin (you will need room to add the vegetables later) and roast in the oven for 30–40 minutes.
- Meanwhile, place all the vegetables, herbs and olive oil in a bowl and mix well, ensuring all the vegetables are thoroughly covered in olive oil. Leave to rest while the chicken starts to cook.
- After the chicken has been in the oven for 30–40 minutes add the vegetable and herb mix to the roasting tray and cook for a further 35–45 minutes, until the chicken and potatoes are cooked.
- Serve with home-made gravy or, in summer, with a salad.

Oven-roasted Italian-style Chicken

Another no-fuss meal, this can be prepared in advance and kept in the fridge until needed. When you are ready, simply pop it in the oven for 20–30 minutes.

Ovenproof dish or roasting tin

4–6 chicken breasts	100g cherry tomatoes
1 small pot of cream cheese	1–2 red peppers, deseeded and thickly sliced
2–3 cloves of garlic, crushed	1–2 red onions, quartered
A small handful of fresh basil leaves (or 1	Olive oil
teaspoon of dried basil)	Balsamic vinegar
1 small pack of pancetta	Sprigs of fresh thyme and rosemary

- Preheat the oven to 180°C/gas mark 4.
- Cut the chicken two-thirds of the way into into each breast. Mix the cream cheese, crushed garlic and basil together and stuff each chicken breast with 1–2 teaspoons of the mixture.
- Wrap pancetta securely around each chicken breast and place on a greased ovenproof dish or roasting tin.
- Add the tomatoes, peppers and onion. Drizzle with olive oil and a touch of balsamic vinegar and add the fresh herbs. If there is any pancetta left, you can cut this into slices and add it to the mix.
- Roast in the oven for 20–30 minutes, until the chicken is cooked.

Chicken and Sun-dried Tomato Casserole

Slow cooker or casserole dish

Olive oil	30g sun-dried tomatoes
I onion	I–2 teaspoons sun-dried tomato purée
2 cloves of garlic, crushed	100ml red wine
I red pepper	300ml chicken stock
300g chicken pieces	I teaspoon oregano
I stick of celery, finely sliced	I bay leaf
I tin of tomatoes	Seasoning to taste

To cook on the hob
- Heat the oil in a pan or casserole dish and fry the onion, garlic and pepper for 2 minutes.
- Add the chicken pieces and stir for 5–8 minutes to help brown them.
- Add all the remaining ingredients. Cover and cook on a low heat for 1–1½ hours.
- Season to taste before serving.

To cook in a slow cooker
- If your slow cooker needs to be preheated, turn it on 15 minutes before using. Refer to your manufacturer's instructions for more information on temperatures for your specific model.
- If you have a sauté facility on your slow cooker, you can brown the chicken in a little oil before adding the onions and garlic.
- If not, simply add all the above ingredients except the olive oil (which is not needed). Make sure the stock is warm when you add it as this will maintain the temperature. Turn your slow cooker to medium heat for 6–8 hours.
- Season to taste before serving.

Creamy Chicken and Mushroom Pasta

Sauté pan and saucepan

300g penne pasta

Olive oil

1 onion, finely chopped (or 2 leeks, finely chopped)

1–2 cloves of garlic, crushed

250g chicken pieces, cooked

125g button mushrooms

1 tub of cream cheese

100–200ml milk

1 teaspoon tarragon

- Place the pasta in a pan of boiling water and start to cook as instructed on the packet.
- Meanwhile, heat the olive oil in a sauté pan. Add the onion, garlic and cooked chicken. Fry until the onions are soft and the chicken is reheated thoroughly.
- Add the mushrooms and cook for a further 3–4 minutes. Remove from the heat.
- Add the cream cheese and milk and stir well until the cream cheese has melted into a sauce. Add the tarragon.
- Drain the pasta and add to the sauce. Stir on a low heat until the sauce is adequately heated. Serve immediately.

Chicken with Creamy Port and Mushroom Sauce

Sauté pan

Olive oil	300ml white wine
4–6 chicken breasts	300ml chicken stock
2–3 cloves of garlic	I heaped teaspoon cornflour
20g butter	Seasoning to taste
I onion, very finely chopped	I teaspoon tarragon
100g mixed wild or chestnut mushrooms,	100ml port
quartered	150ml double cream

- Heat the oil in a large sauté pan and fry the chicken breasts and garlic until the chicken is brown on both sides. Place the chicken on a plate, cover to keep warm and leave to one side for a few minutes – try to retain some of the oil in the pan.
- Return the sauté pan to the heat, melt the butter and fry the onion and mushrooms until they soften, before adding the wine. Allow to reduce slightly before adding the chicken stock.
- Mix the cornflour with a little water then pour onto the stock. Mix thoroughly and allow to thicken/reduce slightly. Season and add the tarragon.
- Return the chicken to the sauté pan and cook for a couple more minutes. Add the port and continue to cook for 5–8 minutes, allowing the flavours to be absorbed and the sauce to reduce slightly. Stir in the double cream, season to taste and cook for a further 2 minutes.
- Serve with rice, mashed or roast potatoes and green vegetables.

Chicken Curry

Sauté pan or casserole dish

Olive oil

1 onion, finely chopped

2–3 cloves of garlic, crushed

1 teaspoon fresh ginger, grated

1 chilli, finely chopped

1 teaspoon coriander seeds

3–4 teaspoons medium curry powder/paste

1 red pepper, finely chopped

4–6 chicken pieces (breast or thigh)

3–4 tomatoes, finely chopped

500–650ml chicken stock

Fresh coriander leaves

2 tablespoons crème fraiche

- Heat oil in the pan or dish and cook the onions, garlic, ginger and chilli for 2–3 minutes to soften. Add the coriander seeds and curry paste or powder. Be careful as this gives off quite a spicy hit and can make your eyes water if you stand directly over the pan.
- Add the red pepper and chicken pieces. Cook the chicken for 4–5 minutes, until starting to brown slightly.
- Add the tomatoes and stock and leave to cook gently on a medium heat for 20–25 minutes.
- Five minutes before serving, add the coriander leaves and stir in the crème fraiche. If you don't have coriander leaves, you can add a touch of green by adding some baby leaf spinach leaves. Just drop them in 5 minutes before serving and allow them to soften naturally.
- Serve on a bed of rice.

Chicken Korma

This is a very easy chicken korma. You can use fresh chicken or leftovers from your Sunday roast. Make sure you cook the chicken thoroughly if you are reheating. This recipe uses natural yoghurt instead of high fat coconut milk. If you like a coconut taste, you could add some grated coconut from a block or try reduced fat coconut milk.

Sauté pan or casserole dish

Olive oil

1 onion

1–2 cloves of garlic, crushed

2.5cm (1in) piece of ginger, finely chopped

½ a fresh chilli, chopped (or ½ teaspoon freeze-dried chillies)

1–2 teaspoons mild curry powder or paste

1 teaspoon turmeric

300g chicken fillet pieces

100ml white wine

200ml water or chicken stock

300ml low fat natural yoghurt

50g almond slices

- Heat the oil in a large sauté pan and fry the onion, garlic and ginger for 2 minutes. Add the chilli, curry powder/paste and turmeric and cook for 1 more minute.
- Add the chicken pieces and cook for 3–4 minutes, turning well.
- Pour on the wine, water/stock and yoghurt and add the almond slices. Mix well. Cook gently on a medium heat for 30 minutes until the chicken is tender and the sauce starts to thicken.
- Serve on a bed of rice.

Tandoori Chicken

You can cheat with this recipe and use a tandoori paste. However, I prefer to make this the more traditional way – there is something deeply satisfying about flinging around herbs and spices when you are cooking. It's also a great way to get the family's attention as the flavours start to waft around the house.

Ovenproof or casserole dish

1 onion, finely chopped	2 teaspoons turmeric
2–3 cloves of garlic, crushed	2–3 teaspoons paprika
1 teaspoon coriander powder	2.5cm (1in) knuckle of ginger, grated
1 teaspoon cayenne pepper	Juice and zest of 1 lemon
1 teaspoon chilli powder (or fresh chillies, finely chopped)	A dash of olive oil
	100g low fat natural yoghurt
1 teaspoon curry powder	4 large chicken pieces

- In an ovenproof dish, mix the onion, garlic, herbs and spices with the lemon juice, zest, olive oil and natural yoghurt.
- Add the chicken pieces and combine thoroughly. For best flavour, leave to marinate in the fridge for a few hours or even overnight.
- When you are ready, preheat the oven to 200°C/gas mark 6 and cook for 30 minutes.
- Serve on a bed of rice.

Note: If you are planning a barbecue, you can marinate the chicken for up to 24 hours in a plastic bag until needed. When you are ready, remove the chicken from the marinade, brush with oil and place on the barbecue to cook. You can reheat the marinade gently and serve as a dressing.

Chicken and Tarragon Risotto

Saucepan or hobproof casserole dish

Olive oil	300g cooked chicken
Knob of butter	300g risotto rice
I onion, finely chopped	200ml white wine
I leek, very finely sliced	500–700ml warm chicken stock
1–2 cloves of garlic, crushed	2 tablespoons tarragon, finely chopped

- Place a splash of olive oil and a knob of butter in the bottom of a saucepan and fry the chopped onion, leek and garlic until translucent. Add the chicken and stir well.
- Add the rice and stir in, ensuring that the rice is completely covered in the oil/butter mixture. Don't let this stick!
- Add the wine and stir thoroughly. The wine will evaporate but will flavour the rice.
- Add the stock (ideally warm or hot stock) a little at a time. Wait until the stock has dissolved each time before adding more. Add the tarragon.
- After 10–15 minutes the rice should be tender (but not soft – it should still have a little bite to it).
- Serve immediately.

Slow Cook Whole Chicken and Vegetables

Slow cooker

1 whole chicken (make sure it fits in your slow cooker!)	2 teaspoons paprika
	2–3 bay leaves
2 onions, roughly chopped	1 teaspoon tarragon
2 carrots, roughly chopped	Seasoning to taste
1–2 leeks, thickly sliced	500ml chicken stock
2 celery sticks, thickly sliced	Water
150g lardons, roughly chopped (optional)	

- If your slow cooker needs to be preheated, turn it on 15 minutes before using. Refer to your manufacturer's instructions for more information on temperatures for your specific model.
- Place the chicken in the slow cooker. Add all the vegetables and lardons, spreading them evenly around and over the chicken.
- Mix the paprika, bay leaves, tarragon, seasoning and chicken stock together and pour over the chicken. Make sure the stock is warm when you add it as this will maintain the temperature.
- Add enough warm water to cover the chicken.
- Cook on high heat for 4–6 hours. You can drain the stock from the chicken, or serve as it is.

Note: Remember, this chicken will not be brown, so if this is unappealing, you can remove it from the slow cooker when it is done and brown it in the oven for 15–20 minutes.

Chicken Chow Mein

Wok or sauté pan

4 chicken breasts or pieces, thinly sliced (you can use cooked chicken)

2–3 teaspoons Chinese five-spice

Olive or sesame oil

2.5cm (1in) knuckle of ginger, finely sliced

1 chilli, finely cut

3–4 cloves of garlic, crushed

2 carrots, finely chopped into thin sticks

4–5 broccoli florets

4–6 spring onions, sliced diagonally

1 pepper, sliced

½ small spring cabbage, shredded

A handful of bean sprouts (optional)

50g mushrooms, sliced

300g noodles

3 tablespoons dry sherry or rice wine

2–3 teaspoons soy sauce

Juice of ½ a lemon

3 tablespoons sweet chilli sauce

- Mix the chicken with the Chinese spices. If using fresh chicken, cook in a wok with a splash of olive oil for a few minutes until browned, then leave to one side until needed.
- Place more oil in the wok and add the ginger, chilli and garlic. Next add your chopped vegetables (apart from the mushrooms) and cook for another 2 minutes, until the vegetables start to wilt slightly, but not go soft.
- Add the chicken, bean sprouts, mushrooms and noodles and cook for 1 more minute.
- Add the sherry or rice wine, soy sauce, lemon juice and sweet chilli sauce and stir well for 1 minute. Serve immediately.

Chicken in Red Wine Sauce

My mum used to make this when we were children and it was always a big favourite of ours. She served it with with mini roast or sauté potatoes and vegetables. You can make a veggie version by substituting Quorn fillets for the chicken fillets.

Slow cooker or casserole dish

Olive oil	1 tin chopped tomatoes
1 onion	200ml red wine
2–3 cloves of garlic, crushed	350ml stock or water
1 red pepper, diced	150g button mushrooms
4 chicken fillets or pieces	1 teaspoon tarragon
2 teaspoons paprika	Seasoning to taste

To cook on the hob
- Heat a dash of olive oil in a large sauté pan or casserole dish and fry the onion and garlic for 2 minutes. Add the pepper and cook for another 2 minutes.
- Add the chicken fillets and paprika. Stir them around, cooking gently for 5 minutes.
- Add all the remaining ingredients. Cover with a lid and cook on a moderate heat for 45 minutes, until the chicken is tender and the sauce has thickened.
- Serve with small roast or sauté potatoes and green vegetables.

To cook in a slow cooker
- If necessary, preheat your slow cooker for 15 minutes while you prepare the vegetables and chicken. Refer to the manufacturer's guidelines for details of your specific model.
- There is no need to brown the chicken breasts, so you can simply add all the ingredients except the olive oil (which is not needed) to the slow cooker. Make sure the stock is warm when you add it as this will maintain the temperature. Cook on high for 3–4 hours or on low for 6 hours.
- Serve with sauté or roast potatoes and green vegetables.

Sweet and Sticky Glazed Chicken

This is a very simple dish recommended by a friend of mine – not sure where she got it from! It takes minutes to prepare but this must be done the night before to allow the flavours to mature.

Mixing bowl and grill

4 chicken breast fillets	1 tablespoon Worcestershire sauce
3 tablespoons maple syrup or honey	1 tablespoon soy sauce
1 tablespoon mustard	2 teaspoons paprika

- Place all the ingredients apart from the chicken in a bowl and mix well.
- Meanwhile, score the fillets with a sharp knife to give the marinade something to hold on to.
- Have a large freezer bag ready as this can get messy! Dip the fillets into the marinade and ensure they are evenly coated, then pop each fillet into the bag.
- Leave in the fridge until the following day when you are ready to cook. (You can speed up this process if you have a vacuum packer or food sealer. The vacuum packer manufacturers claim that 20–30 minutes marinating in a sealed vacuum-packed bag is equivalent to 24 hours in the traditional way.)
- When you are ready to cook, as a precaution, line your grill pan with foil to collect any sticky drips. Grill the chicken gently on both sides adding marinade as you go.
- Serve with salad.

Hearty Chicken Casserole

This is a great standby for using up any leftover chicken or vegetables.

Slow cooker or casserole dish

Olive oil

1 onion, finely chopped

1–2 cloves of garlic, crushed

2 sticks of celery, chopped

1 leek, chopped

2 carrots, sliced

2 potatoes, diced (use sweet potato if you prefer)

300g chicken (use fillets, breast, thighs or chicken pieces – all boneless)

1 tin of tomatoes (or 4–6 ripe fresh tomatoes)

200ml white or red wine (optional)

700ml chicken stock

2 teaspoons paprika

1 bay leaf

To cook in a casserole dish

- Heat the olive oil in a large ovenproof casserole dish and fry the onion and garlic for 2 minutes. Add the celery, leek, carrots and potatoes and cook for 3–4 minutes, stirring occasionally to prevent the vegetables from sticking.
- Add the chicken followed by all the remaining ingredients. Cover with a lid and leave to cook on a very low heat for 1–2 hours.
- Serve with mini jacket potatoes.

To cook in a slow cooker

- If necessary, preheat your slow cooker 15 minutes before using (refer to your manufacturer's guidelines for details of your specific model).
- Place all the ingredients except the olive oil (which is not needed) in your slow cooker. Make sure the stock is warm when you add it as this will maintain the temperature.
- Cook on high for 4–5 hours or on low for 6–8 hours.

Chicken and Mushroom Casserole

Casserole dish

Olive oil

1–2 cloves of garlic

2 leeks, finely chopped

6 spring onions, finely chopped

300g chicken pieces (you can use cooked
   chicken)

175g mushrooms

200ml white wine

300ml chicken stock

1 teaspoon cornflour

1 teaspoon paprika

100g French beans

1 teaspoon dried tarragon (or a handful of
   fresh tarragon)

- Heat the oil in an ovenproof casserole dish and sauté the garlic, leeks and spring onions for 2–3 minutes. Add the chicken and cook for a further 5 minutes.
- Add the mushrooms, wine and chicken stock. Mix the cornflour in a cup with 10ml of water. Stir well then add to the chicken pot.
- Add all the remaining ingredients. If using fresh tarragon, use half now and retain half to add in the last 10 minutes of cooking.
- Cook on a low heat for 45 minutes.

Note: If you prefer a creamier sauce, add some low fat Greek yoghurt or low fat crème fraiche 5 minutes before serving.

Wholesome Chicken Casserole

Casserole dish or slow cooker

Olive oil	500–650ml chicken stock
1 onion	100ml white wine
500g chicken breast (or leftover chicken)	150g mushrooms, quartered
1 pepper, sliced	Sprig of thyme
2 carrots, sliced	1 bay leaf
1 potato, diced	150g sweetcorn
2 sticks of celery, sliced	150g peas

To cook on the hob
- Heat the olive oil and fry the onion, chicken and pepper in a casserole dish or pan and cook gently for 2–3 minutes.
- Add the carrots, potatoes and celery and cook for another 5 minutes.
- Pour over the chicken stock and wine and add the mushrooms, thyme and bay leaf. Cover and cook on a low heat for 1 hour.
- Ten minutes before serving, add the sweetcorn and peas.

To cook in a slow cooker
- If necessary, preheat your slow cooker (refer to your manufacturer's guidelines).
- Place all the ingredients apart from the sweetcorn and peas (which lose their colour in the long, slow cooking process) in your slow cooker. Make sure the stock is warm when you add it as this will maintain the temperature. Cook on a high heat for 4–5 hours or a low heat for 6–8 hours.
- Twenty minutes before serving, add the sweetcorn and peas. You could turn the slow cooker to low or warm and add these while you prepare the rest of the meal.

Chicken and Bacon Casserole

Casserole dish

Olive oil	1 tin of chopped tomatoes
1 red onion, finely chopped	1–2 teaspoons sun-dried tomato paste
2–3 cloves of garlic, crushed	200ml red wine
75g bacon, roughly chopped	1 teaspoon oregano
4–6 chicken pieces	150 ml chicken stock

- Heat the olive oil in a casserole dish and cook the onion, garlic and bacon for 2 minutes before adding the chicken pieces.
- Brown gently but don't allow the bacon to burn.
- Add all the remaining ingredients. Cover and cook on a low/medium heat for 30 minutes. Add more liquid if necessary.

Chicken Chasseur

Casserole dish or slow cooker

Olive oil

25g butter

4–6 chicken pieces

10 small shallots, halved

150g mushrooms, quartered

4–6 ripe tomatoes, skinned and chopped

2–3 teaspoons tomato purée

200ml white wine

450ml chicken stock

1 bay leaf

1–2 teaspoons dried tarragon

Seasoning to taste

To cook on the hob

- Heat the olive oil and butter in a casserole dish and fry the chicken for 2–3 minutes on both sides before adding the shallots and mushrooms. Cook for a further 5–8 minutes.
- Add the tomatoes and tomato purée, followed by the white wine. Cook for 2–3 minutes before gradually adding the stock, bay leaf and tarragon. Season to taste.
- Cover and cook on a low/medium heat for 45 minutes.

To cook in a slow cooker

- If necessary, preheat your slow cooker (refer to your manufacturer's guidelines).
- Place all the ingredients in your slow cooker except the olive oil and butter (which are not needed). Make sure the stock is warm when you add it as this will maintain the temperature.
- Cook on a high heat for 3–4 hours or a low heat for 5–6 hours.

Cajun Chicken Casserole

Casserole dish or slow cooker

Olive oil	1 red pepper, sliced
1 onion	2 teaspoons Cajun spice
2–3 cloves of garlic, crushed	1 teaspoon paprika
1 chilli, finely chopped	2 sticks of celery, sliced
4 chicken pieces (thigh, legs or breast)	1 tin of tomatoes

To cook on the hob
- Heat the oil in a casserole dish and fry the onion, garlic and chilli for 2–3 minutes.
- Add the chicken and red pepper and cook for another 5 minutes.
- Add all the remaining ingredients. Cover and cook on a medium/low heat for 1–1½ hours.

To cook in a slow cooker
- If necessary, preheat your slow cooker (refer to your manufacturer's guidelines).
- Some people like to release the flavours of the spices before adding them to the slow cooker. If you prefer to do this, you can use your slow cooker directly on the hob (if you have this type of cooker) or use a sauté pan. Heat the oil in a pan and fry the onion, garlic and chilli until soft. Brown the chicken for 3–5 minutes (if you prefer this), before placing in the slow cooker.
- Add all the remaining ingredients to your slow cooker and cook on a high heat for 3–4 hours or low heat for 5–6 hours.

Chicken in Creamy Mushroom Sauce

Sauté pan

Olive oil

4 chicken breasts

½ bunch of spring onions

100g chestnut mushrooms

1 teaspoon tarragon

150ml white wine

200 ml crème fraiche

- Heat the oil in a sauté pan and cook the chicken breasts on both sides until cooked through.
- Add the spring onions and mushrooms and cook for a further 5–8 minutes.
- Add the tarragon and wine. Cook for 2–3 minutes before adding the crème fraiche.
- Season before serving.

Leftover Chicken Pie

This is my mum's recipe. Now we have grown up and flown the nest, Mum and Dad have had to adapt to cooking for two instead of four. This meal is made from the leftovers of Mum's Sunday roast, so you can expect to see them tucking into it early in the week!

Sauté pan and pie dish

1 onion, chopped
2 sticks of celery, chopped
75g mushrooms, quartered
200–300g cooked chicken (removed from the bone)
100g cooked ham (optional)

1 can of chicken or mushroom condensed soup
Savoury shortcrust or ready-made puff pastry for pie topping
Beaten egg or milk (for the pastry)
Sesame seeds (optional)
Black pepper to taste

- Preheat the oven to 200°C/gas mark 6.
- Fry the onion in the pan, add the celery, mushrooms, cooked chicken and ham and cook for 3–4 minutes.
- Add the soup and heat for a further 3 minutes.
- Place in a pie dish and cover with savoury shortcrust pastry or, if you are in a hurry, ready-made puff pastry. Use milk or beaten egg to seal and coat the pastry, and finish with a sprinkle of sesame seeds and black pepper.
- Bake in the oven for 30 minutes.

Creamy Chicken, Leek and Ham Pie

This is a similar recipe to the above, but it is made with a combination of Greek yoghurt and Quark. This combination gives the pie a rather decadent feel without the extra calories you would have from adding cream. If you are nervous about using Quark, you can opt for the more calorific double cream.

Sauté pan and pie dish

25g butter

2 leeks, finely sliced

300g cooked chicken (chunky breast or thigh is good)

100g thick ham, cut into chunks

200ml Greek yoghurt (Total is good as it holds its consistency)

100ml Quark (or double cream if you prefer)

1–2 tablespoons wholegrain mustard

2 tablespoons chives, chopped

1 teaspoon dried tarragon

Seasoning to taste

½ a 500g pack of puff pastry

Beaten egg or milk (for the pastry)

Sesame seeds (optional)

- Preheat the oven to 180°C/gas mark 4.
- Heat the butter in the sauté pan and fry the leeks until they start to soften.
- Remove from the heat and add all the remaining ingredients for the filling to the pan. Stir well to ensure the Quark/cream and yoghurt thoroughly coat all the food.
- Season to taste.
- Place the filling in a pie dish and cover with the pastry. Seal and brush with milk or beaten egg. Cover with a sprinkle of sesame seeds and black pepper.
- Bake in the oven for 30 minutes until the pastry is golden.

One Pot Apricot and Ginger Chicken

Roasting tray

Olive oil
500g potatoes
5–7.5cm (2–3in) knuckle of ginger, finely
   chopped
2–3 tablespoons apricot jam
2 teaspoons Dijon mustard
1 tablespoon soy sauce

½ teaspoon ground ginger
2 teaspoons paprika
500g chicken thighs or pieces
2–3 red onions, quartered
1–2 carrots, cut into thick sticks
1–2 parsnips, cut into thick sticks

- Preheat the oven to 200°C/gas mark 6.
- Place a very large ovenproof roasting tray or dish in the oven with a thin layer of oil in the base. (This dish will contain your roast potatoes, chicken thighs and vegetables. If you don't have a very large dish, you can use two smaller roasting trays.)
- Peel and cut the potatoes into small roasting size. Steam or parboil for 10 minutes. Place the drained potatoes in the base of the saucepan. Put the lid on and shake to fluff up the potatoes.
- Meanwhile combine the ginger, apricot jam, mustard, soy sauce, ground ginger and paprika together. If the sauce is very dry, add a touch of olive oil.
- Remove the roasting tray from the oven. Place your potatoes in the tray, allowing them to spit a bit in the hot oil. Ensure they are evenly covered in oil, even if this means most of the oil disappears soaking into the potatoes. Place your chicken thighs on the tray.
- Brush the ginger and apricot jam sauce onto the tops of the chicken thighs, ensuring they are well coated.
- Place the onions, carrots and parsnips around the potatoes and chicken pieces. You can give them a coat of the sauce if you want to.
- Bake in the oven for 45–50 minutes, until the chicken thighs and potatoes are cooked.

One Pot Beef

Braised Oxtail Casserole

Slow cooker

I oxtail, cut into 3–5cm (1½–2in) pieces (ask your butcher to do this)	3 sticks of celery, sliced
	2 carrots, diced
I tablespoon plain flour	I tin of tomatoes, chopped
I tablespoon paprika	2 teaspoons sun-dried tomato paste
Olive oil	300ml red wine
I large onion, sliced	500–700ml beef stock
3 cloves of garlic, crushed	I bay leaf

- Preheat your slow cooker if necessary 15 minutes before using. Refer to the manufacturer's instructions for more information on temperatures for your specific model.
- Run the oxtail pieces under water to moisten them. Mix the flour and paprika together in a bowl. Coat the oxtail pieces with the flour and paprika mix (depending on how many oxtail pieces you have, you may need to use more flour/paprika).
- Heat the olive oil in a sauté pan. Add the oxtail pieces and brown for 5 minutes.
- Transfer these to your slow cooker. Add all the remaining ingredients. Make sure the stock is warm when you add it as this will maintain the temperature of your cooker.
- Turn your slow cooker to high and cook for 6–8 hours.

Traditional Steak and Kidney Pudding

This is a traditional steak and kidney pudding made with suet. It is quite a substantial dish, so is ideal for active, growing families. You can make a similar dish using leftover beef casserole.

Saucepan and steamer or slow cooker

350g beef steak	50g mushrooms, quartered
150g kidneys	150ml red wine
2 tablespoons plain flour	150ml beef stock
1 tablespoon paprika	225g plain flour
Seasoning to taste	2 teaspoons baking powder
Olive oil	100g shredded suet
1 onion	125ml cold water

- Chop the meat into bite-size chunks. Run this under water to moisten.
- Mix the flour and paprika together in a bowl. Season.
- Dip the meat into the flour, ensuring it is well coated.
- Heat the oil in a sauté pan, add the chopped onion and start to soften it. After a couple of minutes add the meat and the mushrooms.
- Cook for 5 minutes, and then add the wine and the stock. Allow this to reduce by half, and then remove from the heat and leave to cool.
- Mix the flour, baking powder and suet in a bowl. Gradually add the cold water until you form a dough. Knead on a floured board and roll out to 1cm (approximately ½in) thickness.
- Line a greased 1 litre pudding basin, ensuring you have enough dough left to make the pastry lid.
- Place the filling into the lined basin. Using a pastry brush, moisten the edges with beaten egg or milk. Place your lid on the top and seal the edges carefully, removing any excess pastry.
- Cover with greaseproof paper and two layers of tin foil. Tie securely with string.
- Place in your steamer for 3 hours, or in the slow cooker, half filled with warm water, on high for 4–6 hours.
- Serve hot with gravy and vegetables.

Slow Cook Beef and Bacon Layer

This is adapted from an old recipe of Mrs Beeton's I discovered. It works perfectly in the slow cooker, though don't use fatty meat or bacon as this can give the dish an unpleasant taste.

Slow cooker

500g brisket of beef, diced

½–1 pack of lean bacon, chopped

1 red onion, sliced

2 sticks of celery, sliced

1 large carrot, sliced

2 potatoes, sliced

500ml hot beef stock

200ml red wine

1 teaspoon thyme

½ teaspoon allspice

Seasoning to taste

- Preheat your slow cooker if necessary 15 minutes before using. Refer to the manufacturer's instructions for more information on temperatures for your specific model.
- Prepare the meat and vegetables.
- Layer the beef, vegetable slices and bacon in your slow cooker, starting with a layer of vegetables as these take longest to cook.
- Thoroughly mix the hot beef stock with the wine, herbs and seasoning.
- Pour over the meat and vegetable mix, ensuring it is evenly covered.
- Cook on high for 5–6 hours.

Beef and Cranberry Casserole

Slow cooker or casserole dish

500g stewing beef

1–2 tablespoons flour

2 teaspoons allspice

Olive oil

2–3 cloves of garlic, finely chopped

1 onion, finely chopped

2 sticks of celery, sliced

1 large carrot, diced

1 sweet potato, diced

200g cranberries (fresh or frozen)

Zest and juice of 1 orange

200ml red wine

650ml beef stock

Seasoning to taste

To cook on the hob

- Cut the beef into chunks. If necessary, moisten with a little water. Mix the flour and allspice together. Dip the beef into the flour mix, ensuring it is evenly coated.
- Heat the olive oil in your casserole dish and fry the garlic and onion until they are soft.
- Add the beef and cook until it is starting to brown all over.
- Add the remaining vegetables (not the fruit) and allow to sweat for 5 minutes.
- Add all the remaining ingredients. Cover and cook on a low/medium heat for 45 minutes–1 hour.
- Season before serving.

To cook in the slow cooker

- Preheat your slow cooker if necessary 15 minutes before using. Refer to the manufacturer's instructions for more information on temperatures for your specific model.
- Cut the beef into chunks. If necessary, moisten with a little water. Mix the flour and allspice together. Dip the beef into the flour mix, ensuring it is evenly coated.
- Using your slow cooker pan or a sauté pan, heat the oil and cook the onion, garlic and beef until browned and the onions start to soften.
- Return this to the slow cooker and add all the remaining ingredients. Make sure the stock is warm when you add it as this will maintain the temperature. Turn your cooker to high for 6 hours or low for 8 hours.
- Season before serving.

Corned Beef Hash Pie

This was a real family favourite during the seventies and eighties. We are now seeing a revival of many of these 'budget' foods so I could not resist including this. If you plan your meals in advance, you could make double the amount of mashed potato the night before, and you will have the basis for a really quick and easy meal. This also makes a perfect lunch served with baked beans!

Saucepan and pie dish

400g potatoes, cooked and mashed	1 onion, finely chopped
100g butter	1 teaspoon Worcestershire sauce (or 2
200g plain flour	teaspoons tomato sauce if you prefer)
1 can of corned beef	Seasoning to taste

- Preheat the oven to 200°C/gas mark 6.
- Cook and mash your potatoes. Meanwhile, make your pastry. I normally use my electric food processor for this, but you can do it by hand. Mix the butter with the flour, using your fingertips to create a texture similar to breadcrumbs. Add *cold* water, a little at a time, to form a ball of firm dough. Place the pastry in the fridge for at least 5 minutes to cool.
- On a floured board, roll out the pastry to the desired thickness to line your pie dish (I use a 25cm (10in) pie dish). Trim.
- Mash the corned beef and add the mashed potato, chopped onion and Worcestershire or tomato sauce. Season well.
- Place this in the pie dish. If you have some pastry left you can add a lid, or a lattice top, whatever you prefer.
- Bake in the oven for 25–35 minutes until golden.

Beef, Vegetable and Horseradish Casserole

You could cook this in a casserole dish on the hob or in the oven, but the slow cooker will give you very tender meat.

Slow cooker

500g brisket of beef, cubed	2 potatoes, diced
25g flour	1–2 parsnips, diced
Olive oil	30g pearl barley
1 onion, diced	2 level tablespoons horseradish sauce
½ swede, cubed	650ml beef stock
2–3 carrots, sliced	

- Preheat your slow cooker if necessary 15 minutes before using. Refer to the manufacturer's instructions for more information on temperatures for your specific model.
- Chop the brisket into cubes. Dip the beef into the flour ensuring it is evenly coated.
- Heat the oil in your slow cooker or in a sauté pan if you don't have a sauté facility in your slow cooker. Add the beef and onion and cook until the onion starts to soften and the beef browns.
- Transfer if necessary back to the slow cooker. Add all the remaining ingredients. Make sure the stock is warm when you add it as this will maintain the temperature of your cooker. Stir well.
- Turn your cooker to low for 8 hours.

Slow Cook Brisket and Vegetables

Slow cooker

500g brisket of beef

Olive oil

1 large red onion, sliced

40g lardons, finely chopped

2 carrots, sliced

1 parsnip, sliced

2 celery sticks, sliced

400ml beef stock

300ml red wine

2 teaspoons paprika

1 teaspoon dried parsley

Seasoning to taste

1 bouquet garni

- If your slow cooker has a sauté facility, turn it to high, heat the oil and brown the brisket. Alternatively, heat the oil in a sauté pan and brown the brisket before placing in the preheated slow cooker.
- Add all the remaining ingredients to the slow cooker. Make sure the stock is warm when you add it as this will maintain the temperature of your cooker.
- Turn your cooker to low and cook for 6–8 hours.

Slow Cook Beef Roast with Red Wine and Cranberries

I discovered this recipe on a slow cook blog. It is really simple to prepare and creates a very tender joint.

Slow cooker

Beef joint	300ml red wine
Butter or olive oil	1 tablespoon Worcestershire sauce
1–2 tablespoons flour	2 tablespoons soy sauce
1–2 tablespoons dried onion	3 tablespoons maple syrup
Sea salt and black pepper to taste	150g cranberries
3 cloves of garlic, crushed	

- Preheat your slow cooker if necessary 15 minutes before using. Refer to the manufacturer's guidelines for details of your specific model.
- Rub the joint with a little butter or olive oil. Mix the flour, onion, salt and pepper together. Rub this all over the joint, ensuring that it is thoroughly coated.
- Place the joint in the slow cooker and set to low.
- Mix all the remaining ingredients together, apart from the cranberries, and pour the liquid into the slow cooker. Add the cranberries.
- Cover and cook on low for 8–10 hours, until tender.

Slow Cook Beef and Ale Stew with Herb Dumplings

You need to prepare the herb dumplings about 45 minutes before you are ready to serve the stew, to give them time to cook. If you like, you can make them in advance and keep them in the fridge until you need them.

Slow cooker

For the stew

1–2 tablespoons plain flour

Seasoning to taste

400–500g beef stewing steak, cut into chunks

Olive oil (for browning the meat)

1 red onion, finely chopped

1 tablespoon redcurrant jelly

600ml ale

1 leek, finely sliced

2–3 carrots, sliced

1 parsnip, sliced

125g button mushrooms, whole

200ml beef stock (if more liquid is needed)

1 bay leaf

1 teaspoon caraway seeds

For the herb dumplings

100g self-raising flour

50g suet

2–3 teaspoons mixed herbs

4 tablespoons water

- Preheat your slow cooker 15 minutes before using. Refer to the manufacturer's instructions for more information on temperatures for your specific model.
- Place 1–2 tablespoons of flour in a bowl and mix in the seasoning. Dip the beef chunks in the flour mixture ensuring they are thoroughly coated.
- If you prefer to brown your meat, you can heat a little oil in the slow cooker if you have a sauté facility, or in a sauté pan on the hob. Fry the beef and onion until the beef starts to brown.
- Add the redcurrant jelly and, when it is melted, add the ale.
- Add all the remaining ingredients. Add the beef stock if more liquid if needed. Make sure the stock is warm when you add it as this will maintain the temperature of your cooker. Turn your slow cooker to low and cook for 6–8 hours.

To make the herb dumplings

- Thoroughly mix the flour, suet and herbs together. Add the water gradually, a little at a time, to form a firm dough.
- Shape the dough into small balls and place these on top of the stew. Cover and leave for 30–45 minutes, until the dumplings fluff up.
- Serve when the dumplings are ready.

Beef Casserole

Slow cooker or casserole dish

A dash of olive oil
1 onion, chopped
1–2 cloves of garlic, crushed
300–400g beef stewing steak, chopped into
   chunks
2 sticks of celery, chopped
2 leeks, sliced
2 carrots, sliced

2 potatoes, chopped
100ml red wine
750ml water or beef stock
3 teaspoons paprika
2–3 bay leaves
50–75g pearl barley
2–3 teaspoons tomato purée
Seasoning to taste

To cook on the hob

- Heat the oil in a large sauté pan or casserole dish and fry the onion, garlic and beef for 5 minutes. Add the other vegetables and stir gently for 3–4 minutes to help soften them.
- Add all the remaining ingredients and heat gently. Cook slowly for 1–1½ hours. Stir occasionally and add more liquid if necessary.

To cook in a slow cooker

- Preheat your slow cooker if necessary as directed in the manufacturer's instructions.
- Using your slow cooker pan or a sauté pan, heat the oil and fry the onion, garlic and beef until the beef is browned and the onions start to soften.
- Place in the slow cooker and add all the remaining ingredients. Make sure the stock is warm when you add it as this will maintain the temperature. Turn your cooker to high for 6 hours, or low for 8 hours.

Beef and Mushroom in Red Wine

This can be cooked on the hob, in the oven or in a slow cooker.

Slow cooker or casserole dish

50g plain flour

3 teaspoons paprika

450g stewing steak, cut into cubes

Olive oil

1 onion, sliced

2 cloves of garlic, crushed

2 leeks, sliced

2 carrots, sliced

1 parsnip, sliced

2 tablespoons redcurrant jelly

200ml red wine

550ml beef stock

125g button mushrooms

To cook on the hob or in the oven
- If you are cooking this in the oven, preheat the oven to 170°C/gas mark 3.
- Mix the flour and paprika together in a bowl and add the beef steak, ensuring it is thoroughly coated in the mixture.
- Heat the olive oil in an ovenproof casserole dish or sauté pan and fry the onion and leeks for 2 minutes.
- Add the beef and cook for a further 3–4 minutes, stirring well to prevent it sticking. Add the carrots and parsnip and sweat these for another 3–4 minutes with the lid on.
- Add the redcurrant jelly and stir well. Gradually add the wine, beef stock and mushrooms.
- Cover and cook gently on a low heat or in the oven for 1–1½ hours. The lower the heat and the longer this cooks, the more tender the beef will be. However, you may have to add more liquid as this will evaporate.

To cook in a slow cooker
- Preheat your slow cooker if necessary as directed in the manufacturer's instructions.
- If you prefer to brown your meat first, you can use your slow cooker pan or a sauté pan, heat the oil and cook the onion, garlic and beef until browned and the onion starts to soften.
- Return everything to the slow cooker and add all the remaining ingredients. Make sure the stock is warm when you add it as this will maintain the temperature. Turn your cooker to high for 4–5 hours, or low for 6–8 hours.

Daube of Beef

Daube of beef is a traditional French stew normally cooked in various stages over a period of days to make the most of the flavours. You can speed up the marinating process by using a vacuum packer, which seals the flavours. This luxurious stew is well worth the preparation. Although traditionally it would have been made with white wine, I think red goes much better with beef. However, the choice is yours.

Slow cooker

450ml red wine	2 sticks of cinnamon
2 tablespoons brandy	2 bay leaves
2 cloves of garlic, finely chopped	2 teaspoons paprika
Sprigs of rosemary and thyme	2 carrots, diced
1 orange, unpeeled, cut into 6 segments	1 leek, finely diced
3–4 small red onions, quartered	1 tin of chopped tomatoes
6–8 sun-dried tomatoes (in oil)	150g button mushrooms, whole
500g beef, cubed	A handful of olives

- Place the wine, brandy, garlic, herbs, orange, onions and sun-dried tomatoes in your slow cooker pan or bowl and combine well. Add the beef and cover. Leave in the fridge overnight to allow the flavours to be absorbed.
- Next morning, remove the beef from the fridge.
- Preheat your slow cooker if necessary. Refer to the manufacturer's instructions for more information on temperatures for your specific model.
- Add all the remaining ingredients to the slow cooker apart from the olives.
- Turn your slow cooker to low for 8 hours.
- Half an hour before serving, add the olives.
- Remove the cinnamon sticks and orange, season and serve.

Beef Goulash

Slow cooker or casserole dish

Olive oil

1 red onion, finely sliced

1–2 cloves of garlic, crushed

2 red peppers, finely sliced

500g beef stewing steak, cut into chunks

1 tin chopped tomatoes

1–2 teaspoons tomato purée

4 teaspoons paprika

200ml red wine

200ml beef stock

A handful of freshly chopped parsley

150ml crème fraiche or Greek-style yoghurt

To cook on the hob

- Heat the olive oil in a pan and fry the onion, garlic and peppers for 2–3 minutes before adding the beef. Cook for 5 minutes until browned.
- Add the tomatoes, tomato purée and paprika and stir, before adding the wine, beef stock and half the chopped parsley.
- Cook on medium heat for 35 minutes, checking occasionally to adjust the liquid if necessary.
- Just prior to serving add the remaining chopped parsley and stir in the crème fraiche (or Greek-style yoghurt if you prefer; I find Total Greek Yoghurt is the best).

To cook in a slow cooker

- Preheat your slow cooker if necessary as directed in the manufacturer's instructions.
- Using your slow cooker pan or a sauté pan, heat the oil and cook the onion, garlic and beef until browned and the onions start to soften. (You can ignore this part if you don't want to brown the meat.)
- Return the onion, garlic and beef to the slow cooker and add all the remaining ingredients apart from the crème fraiche and parsley. Make sure the stock is warm when you add it as this will maintain the temperature. Turn your slow cooker to high for 4 hours, or low for 6 hours.
- Just prior to serving add the chopped parsley and stir in the crème fraiche (or Greek-style yoghurt if you prefer; I find Total Greek Yoghurt is the best).

Beef Stroganoff

Sauté pan

Olive oil

1 onion, finely chopped

2–3 cloves of garlic, crushed

500g lean beef steak chunks

300g mushrooms, sliced

2–3 teaspoons Dijon mustard

2 teaspoons fresh tarragon

200ml white wine

150ml fromage frais

- Heat the oil in a large sauté pan and fry the onion and garlic for 5 minutes. Add the beef and cook for another 5 minutes, ensuring it is evenly browned.
- Add the mushrooms, mustard and tarragon; stir well, before adding the wine. Some of this will evaporate as you continue to cook for 10–15 minutes.
- Just before serving, remove from the heat and stir in the fromage frais to form a creamy sauce.
- Serve on a bed of white rice.

Beef and Stout Stew

Slow cooker or casserole dish

500g stewing beef

2 tablespoons plain flour

1 tablespoon olive oil

1 onion, chopped

2 cloves of garlic, crushed

2 carrots, sliced

2 potatoes, cubed

350ml stout or Guinness

4 sprigs of thyme

A pinch of cayenne pepper

200ml water or beef stock

Seasoning to taste

To cook on the hob

- Dip the beef in water and then roll it in the flour. Leave to one side.
- Heat the oil in a large casserole dish and fry the onion and garlic for 2 minutes.
- Add the carrots and potatoes and cook for a further 5 minutes, stirring occasionally to prevent the vegetables from sticking.
- Add the floured beef and cook for a further 2 minutes, stirring continuously. Add the stout, thyme, cayenne pepper and water or stock. Season to taste.
- Place a lid on the dish and cook gently on a low heat for 1–2 hours depending on taste; the longer you cook it the tenderer the meat. You may need to add more liquid if cooking for longer periods.

To cook in a slow cooker

- Preheat your slow cooker if necessary as directed in the manufacturer's instructions.
- If you prefer to brown your meat first, you can use your slow cooker pan or a sauté pan, heat the oil and cook the onion, garlic and floured beef until browned and the onion starts to soften.
- Return everything to the slow cooker and add all the remaining ingredients. Make sure the stock is warm when you add it as this will maintain the temperature. Turn your cooker to high for 4–6 hours, depending on taste. You may need to add more liquid if cooking for longer periods.

Spaghetti Bolognese

This recipe can be made using a 'cheat' ingredient of bolognese or pasta sauce instead of the tin of tomatoes.

Sauté pan

Olive oil

1 onion, finely chopped

2–3 cloves of garlic, finely chopped

1 pepper, finely chopped (optional)

400g minced beef

150ml red wine

75g mushrooms, finely chopped (optional)

1 tin of chopped tomatoes

Dried mixed herbs to taste

Seasoning to taste

1 teaspoon sugar (optional)

- Heat the oil in a pan and fry the onion and garlic until soft and translucent. Add the pepper if using.
- Add the mince and cook until brown. Add the wine and mushrooms and cook for 2 more minutes.
- Add the chopped tinned or fresh tomatoes (or 'cheat' pasta sauce), stirring well. Add the herbs and season to taste. Some people like to add a teaspoon of sugar to their bolognese sauce – adjust the amount to suit your palate. Leave the sauce to simmer on a low heat for 10–15 minutes.
- Serve on a bed of cooked spaghetti and garnish with grated Parmesan.

Traditional Beef Lasagne

Saucepan and ovenproof dish

For the bolognese sauce
Olive oil
I onion, finely chopped
2–3 cloves of garlic, finely chopped
I pepper, finely chopped (optional)
500g lean minced beef
150ml red wine
75g mushrooms, finely chopped (optional)
I tin of chopped tomatoes
Dried mixed herbs to taste
Seasoning to taste

For the white sauce
25g butter
I tablespoon plain flour or cornflour
500–750ml milk
½ teaspoon mustard (optional)
Black pepper to taste

Lasagne sheets (ensure it says no precook required on pack)
Grated cheese to garnish

- Preheat the oven to 200°C/gas mark 6.
- Heat the oil in a pan and fry the onion and garlic until soft and translucent. Add the pepper if using.
- Add the mince and cook until brown. Add the wine and mushrooms and cook for 2 more minutes.
- Add the chopped tinned or fresh tomatoes (or 'cheat' pasta sauce), stirring well. Add the herbs and season to taste. Leave to cook gently for 10–15 minutes.
- While the bolognese sauce is cooking, make the white sauce. Melt the butter gently in a saucepan on medium heat (not high!). Add the flour or cornflour and stir well with a wooden spoon. Add the milk a little at a time, continuing to stir to avoid lumps.
- Switch now to a balloon whisk. Continue to stir over a medium heat until the sauce begins to thicken. The balloon whisk will also help eradicate any lumps that may have materialised. Add more milk as necessary to get the desired thickness. The sauce should be the thickness of custard.
- Add the mustard and season with black pepper.
- Place a layer of bolognese mix in the bottom of your lasagne dish, and then add a thin layer of white sauce, followed by a layer of lasagne sheets. Continue layering in this way, finishing with a topping of white sauce. Do not overfill your dish as the sauce may spill out during the cooking.

- Grate some cheese over the white sauce, season and sprinkle with some Italian herbs, before placing the lasagne in the oven for 30–40 minutes.
- Serve with salad and garlic bread.

Chilli Con Carne

A firm family favourite, this can be served on a bed of rice, used as a filling in wraps and tortillas, or as a topping for jacket potatoes. You can double up the recipe and freeze half to make a meal for another day.

Sauté pan

Olive oil	400g lean minced beef (or drained of fat)
I onion, finely chopped	200ml red wine
I–2 cloves garlic, crushed	I tin of chopped tomatoes
I red pepper, chopped	I tin of red kidney beans
100g mushrooms, quartered	I teaspoon chilli powder
I–2 chopped chillies (depending on desired flavour)	I teaspoon paprika
	Seasoning to taste

- Heat the oil in a large sauté pan and fry the onion, garlic, pepper and mushrooms for 1–2 minutes. Add the chopped chillies and cook for 1 more minute. Add the mince and cook until brown. The mixture should be cooking in its own liquid, but if it seems a little dry add a small amount of the wine.
- Add the wine, tomatoes, kidney beans, chilli powder and paprika. Season to taste. Allow to simmer gently for 20 minutes. The longer this is cooked, the thicker the sauce will be.
- Serve as desired.

Beef and Mushroom Cobbler

Casserole dish

For the beef casserole
450g stewing steak, cut into cubes
50g plain flour
3 teaspoons paprika
Olive oil
1 onion
2 leeks, sliced
2 tablespoons redcurrant jelly
200ml red wine
350ml beef stock
125g button mushrooms

For the cobbler/scone topping
100g self-raising flour
75ml natural yoghurt
2 tablespoons olive oil
A handful of chopped parsley

- Place the beef steak in a bowl and coat with the flour and paprika.
- Heat the olive oil in an ovenproof casserole dish and fry the onion and leeks for 2 minutes.
- Add the beef and cook for a further 3–4 minutes, stirring well to avoid it sticking.
- Add the redcurrant jelly and stir well. Gradually add the wine, beef stock and mushrooms.
- Cover and cook gently on a low heat for 20 minutes.
- Meanwhile, preheat the oven to 200°C/gas mark 6.
- Place the flour in a bowl and add the yoghurt, oil and chopped parsley. Mix to form a soft dough. Place on a floured board and shape into individual balls. Flatten slightly.
- Remove the beef casserole from the hob, but keep it in the ovenproof dish. Place the scones on top of the casserole, forming a circle or completely covering the top of the casserole.
- Bake in the oven for 20–30 minutes until the scones are golden and fluffy.
- Serve immediately.

Cottage Pie

This is real comfort food that can be prepared in advance. Kids love it!

Ovenproof dish

800g potatoes, cut into rough chunks

4 carrots, 2 roughly chopped and 2 cut into small cubes

I onion, chopped

400g lean minced beef (or drained of fat)

75g mushrooms, sliced (optional)

100ml red wine (optional)

I teaspoon yeast extract (Marmite or similar)

200–300ml meat gravy (or vegetable gravy if using veggie mince)

Seasoning to taste

Worcestershire sauce

25g butter

75g mature Cheddar

A sprinkle of paprika

- Preheat the oven to 180°C/gas mark 4.
- Place the potatoes and the 2 roughly chopped carrots in a steamer and cook until soft.
- Meanwhile, in a large sauté pan, fry the onions for 1–2 minutes before adding the mince.
- Cook until the mince is brown before adding the 2 cubed carrots, the mushrooms and the wine.
- Dissolve the yeast extract in the hot gravy before adding to the mince. Cook for 20 minutes until the mince is tender and the gravy is reduced to the desired consistency. Season to taste and add the Worcestershire sauce.
- Mash the potato and carrots together. Add the butter and two thirds of the Cheddar. Mix thoroughly.
- Place the mince in a deep baking dish and spoon the mash over the top. Be careful not to overfill the dish. Press down gently with a fork. Top with the remaining grated cheese and a sprinkle of paprika.
- Bake in the oven for 30 minutes.

Spicy Beef and Bean Casserole

Slow cooker

1–2 tablespoons plain flour	2 carrots, sliced
1 teaspoon ground ginger	1 sweet potato
500g stewing beef, cut into chunks	1 tin of red kidney beans
Seasoning to taste	1–2 teaspoons chilli powder (depending on
1 red onion, sliced	personal taste)
2 cloves of garlic, crushed	1 tablespoon Worcestershire sauce
1 red pepper, sliced	50ml red wine vinegar
1 tin of tomatoes	300ml beef stock

- Preheat your slow cooker if necessary as directed in the manufacturer's instructions.
- Mix the flour and ground ginger together and season. Dip the beef chunks into the flour ensuring they are evenly covered.
- If you would like to brown the meat, you can do so in a sauté pan or in your slow cooker if it is hobproof. Heat a little olive oil, add the onion and garlic and brown the beef. (You may omit this step if you wish.)
- Place all the ingredients in the slow cooker, ensuring they are evenly distributed. Make sure the stock is warm when you add it as this will maintain the temperature of your cooker.
- Cover and cook slowly on high for 4–6 hours or low for 6–8 hours.

One Pot Pork

Slow Cook Sweet and Sour Pork

Slow cooker

750g pork, cubed or cut into strips

1 red onion, sliced

3–4 cloves of garlic, crushed

1 yellow pepper, sliced

2.5cm (1in) knuckle of ginger, finely chopped

75ml white wine

75ml red wine vinegar

50g brown sugar

100ml water

100ml pineapple juice

3–4 tablespoons soy sauce

2 tablespoons tomato ketchup

- Preheat your slow cooker if necessary as directed in the manufacturer's instructions.
- You can brown the pork if you prefer, before placing it in the slow cooker, or simply add all the ingredients to the slow cooker. Make sure the water is warm when you add it as this will maintain the temperature.
- Stir well to ensure the ingredients are evenly distributed. Turn the slow cooker to low and cook for 8 hours.
- Once cooked, if you prefer a thicker sauce, mix 2 teaspoons cornflour with 50ml water, combine well and then add to the pork mixture. Turn the slow cooker to high and cook for 30 minutes.
- Serve on a bed of rice.

Pork Meatball and Tomato Casserole

You can prepare the meatballs in advance and freeze them until needed.

Casserole dish or slow cooker

For the pork meatballs

400g pork mince

2 tablespoons basil, chopped

2 cloves garlic, crushed

2–3 sun-dried tomatoes, chopped

1 teaspoon olive oil

1 teaspoon soy sauce

For the tomato sauce

1 red onion, finely chopped

2 sticks of celery, finely chopped

1 red pepper, diced

1–2 carrots, diced

1 tin of tomatoes, chopped

30g sun-dried tomatoes, chopped

200ml red wine (optional)

350–500ml vegetable stock or water

1 bay leaf

3 teaspoons paprika

1 teaspoon oregano

To make the pork meatballs

• Simply combine all the ingredients in a bowl and mix thoroughly.

• Form into small balls and place on a baking sheet. Cover the balls with a sheet of cling film and store in the fridge for 30 minutes while you get on with making the sauce.

• Alternatively, you can freeze the balls. I normally place the baking tray in the freezer until the meatballs are firm, before taking them off the tray and placing them in a freezer bag. This way they won't stick together and you can pull out as many as you need.

To cook on the hob

• Fry the meatballs until brown. Remove from the pan and place on one side. Add all the tomato sauce ingredients to the pan and cook on a low/medium heat for 10 minutes.

• Add the meatballs, turn the heat to low and cook gently for 30–45 minutes.

To cook in a slow cooker

• Preheat your slow cooker if necessary as directed in the manufacturer's instructions.

• Place all the tomato sauce ingredients in the slow cooker and set to high. Make sure the stock is warm when you add it as this will maintain the temperature.

• Meanwhile, fry the meatballs on the hob until they are brown.

• Add the meatballs to the slow cooker and cook for 4 hours.

• Serve with spaghetti.

Sausage Cobbler

Ovenproof dish

For the sausage casserole
8 sausages
75g pancetta or lardons (optional)
I red onion, sliced
2 cloves of garlic, crushed
100g button mushrooms
250ml red wine
I tin of chopped tomatoes
2–3 teaspoons sun-dried tomato purée
I teaspoon Italian herbs

For the cobbler topping
50g butter
150g self-raising flour
125ml milk
50g mature Cheddar

- Preheat the oven to 200°C/gas mark 6.
- Place the sausages, pancetta or lardons (if you are using these), onion and garlic in an ovenproof dish, drizzle with olive oil and bake in the oven for 15 minutes. Alternatively, sauté them on the hob until the sausages are brown. I normally add the mushrooms for the last couple of minutes to start to soften them and release the flavour.
- Meanwhile prepare the cobbler topping. Rub the butter into the flour with your fingertips. Gradually add the milk to form a firm dough. Roll out onto a floured surface and cut into round scones.
- Once the sausages are brown, transfer them (if necessary) to the ovenproof dish. Add the wine, tomatoes, purée and herbs. Mix well.
- Place the scones around the edge of the sausage mix. Coat with milk, then sprinkle with grated cheese.
- Bake in the oven for 30 minutes, until the scones are golden.

Bacon and Egg Potato Salad

I love potato salad, especially on summer days and picnics. It is great for using up leftover potatoes and any spare bits and pieces in the fridge. You can add cucumber, celery, fresh peas or even bits of chicken. If you like it spicy, why not add some chopped chillies or even a dash of Tabasco sauce.

Serving bowl

400g cooked potatoes, cubed or if using new potatoes, halved

4–6 rashers of bacon, cooked and cut into chunks

1 onion, finely chopped

3 hard-boiled eggs cut into chunks

1–2 tablespoons fresh mint, finely chopped

A handful of fresh chives, finely chopped

Juice of ½ lemon

2–3 tablespoons mayonnaise, ideally low fat

Seasoning to taste

- Place the chopped cooked potatoes in a large bowl. Add all the remaining ingredients and combine until evenly mixed.
- Season to taste before serving.

Bacon, Cannellini and Vegetable Casserole

Slow cooker or casserole dish

Olive oil

1 large red onion, finely chopped

2 cloves of garlic

1 pack of lean bacon, roughly chopped

1 pepper, diced

2–3 carrots, diced

2–3 sticks of celery, diced

1–2 sweet potatoes, diced

1 tin of chopped tomatoes,

6–10 sun-dried tomatoes (in oil)

1 tin of cannellini beans

600ml vegetable stock

2 teaspoons paprika

1 teaspoon thyme

1 bay leaf

2–3 handfuls of baby leaf spinach

To cook on the hob

• Heat the oil in a casserole dish and fry the onion and garlic until the onion starts to soften.

• Add the bacon and pepper, and cook for 2 minutes. Add the carrots, celery and sweet potato. Allow to sweat for 5 minutes before adding the tomatoes and beans.

• Add the stock, paprika and herbs and leave on a low heat for 1–1½ hours or medium heat for 30–40 minutes.

• Before serving, add the spinach. Leave for 5 minutes, season and serve.

To cook in a slow cooker

• Turn your slow cooker to the hot or sauté setting, heat the oil and fry the onion and garlic until the onion starts to soften.

• Add the bacon and pepper, and cook for 2 minutes.

• Add all the remaining ingredients apart from the spinach. Make sure the stock is warm when you add it as this will maintain the temperature of your cooker. Cook on a low heat for 6–8 hours.

• Before serving, add the spinach. Leave for 5 minutes, season and serve.

Slow and Easy Italian-style Pork Chops

Slow cooker

4–6 boneless pork chops	I tin of chopped tomatoes
I red onion, sliced	200ml red wine
2 cloves of garlic, crushed	75g button mushrooms, whole
I red pepper, diced	I teaspoon oregano
6–8 sun-dried tomatoes	

- Preheat your slow cooker as directed in the manufacturer's instructions.
- Place all the ingredients in the slow cooker. Stir well to ensure the ingredients are evenly distributed.
- Turn your cooker to low and cook for 4–6 hours.

Slow Cook Gammon

My mum is a big fan of gammon and likes to cook this on special occasions.

Slow cooker

I gammon joint	2–3 sticks of cinnamon
2 tablespoons honey	I teaspoon nutmeg
20–30 cloves	5cm (2in) knuckle of ginger, roughly chopped
I litre of apple juice	I orange, peeled and quartered

- Preheat your slow cooker if necessary as directed in the manufacturer's instructions.
- Rub the honey into the skin of the gammon joint. Place the cloves into the skin – you may need to pierce the skin with a needle beforehand if the skin is tough.
- Place the gammon in the slow cooker. Pour in the apple juice. Add the cinnamon, nutmeg, ginger and orange.
- Cook the gammon on a low heat for 8–10 hours.
- Delicious sliced and served with parsley sauce and sauté potatoes.

Slow Cook Pork Chops

Slow cooker

4–6 boneless pork chops	200ml red wine
I red onion, finely chopped	50ml soy sauce
2 cloves of garlic	2 teaspoons paprika
2.5cm (1in) knuckle of ginger, chopped	2 tablespoons brown sugar

- Preheat your slow cooker as directed in the manufacturer's instructions.
- Place the pork chops, onion, garlic and ginger in the slow cooker.
- Mix the wine, soy sauce, paprika and sugar together before pouring over the chops.
- Cover and leave on low heat for 4–6 hours. Serve with mashed potato and seasonal greens.

Sausage and Baked Bean Bake

This is a really simple dish. Kids love it as it offers the sweetness of the beans along with the temptation of the sausages – perfect for bonfire night!

Casserole dish or ovenproof dish

8 sausages	I tin of baked beans
I red onion	I tin of chopped tomatoes
1–2 cloves of garlic (optional)	A splash of Worcestershire sauce
75g lardons (optional)	Chopped fresh thyme
Olive oil	

- Preheat the oven to 180°C/gas mark 4.
- Place the sausages, onion, garlic and lardons (if using) in an ovenproof dish, drizzle with olive oil and bake in the oven for 20 minutes.
- Meanwhile, mix the baked beans, tomatoes, Worcestershire sauce and fresh thyme together.
- Add the baked bean mixture to the cooked sausages and mix together thoroughly. Return the dish to the oven and cook for a further 20 minutes before serving.

Sweet and Sour Pork Stir-fry

Wok and mixing bowl

2 teaspoons sesame oil

2 tablespoons light soy sauce

2 tablespoons tomato purée

1 tablespoon brown sugar

1 x 400g tin of pineapple chunks in natural juice

2 teaspoons cornflour

150ml stock

2 tablespoons rice wine or white wine vinegar

Olive oil

400g pork, trimmed and cubed

2 cloves of garlic, crushed

2 peppers, sliced

2.5–5cm (1–2in) knuckle of ginger, thinly sliced

6 spring onions, sliced

- Place the sesame oil, soy sauce, tomato purée, sugar, pineapple chunks and juice, cornflour, stock and rice wine/wine vinegar in a bowl.
- Heat the oil in a wok or sauté pan and cook the pork chunks for 5 minutes, until coloured.
- Add the garlic, peppers, ginger and spring onions and cook for another 5 minutes.
- Pour on the sauce and continue to cook for another 2–3 minutes.
- Serve on a bed of rice or noodles.

Pork Loin in Red Wine Sauce

Slow cooker

Pork loin

1–2 tablespoons of redcurrant jelly

3 cloves of garlic, crushed

1 red onion, finely chopped

2 glasses of red wine

• Preheat your slow cooker as directed in the manufacturer's instructions.

• Mix the redcurrant jelly and garlic together. Spread this over the pork loin.

• Place in the slow cooker. Add the onion and pour the wine down the side of the loin, taking care not to wash off the redcurrant jelly from the top of the loin.

• Cook on a low setting for 4–6 hours.

• To serve, slice the loin and drizzle with red wine sauce.

Slow Cook Christmas Gammon

This is a variation on my mum's traditional slow cook gammon. You get a lovely Christmassy flavour with this, so enjoy!

Slow cooker and roasting tray

1 gammon joint	2 star anise
2 red onions, halved (still in skins)	2 teaspoons peppercorns
2 oranges, unpeeled and quartered	Cloves
2 sticks of cinnamon	3 tablespoons red wine
400ml mulled wine	Zest of 1 orange
1 fennel bulb, halved	2 tablespoons redcurrant jelly

- Preheat your slow cooker as directed in the manufacturer's instructions.
- Place the gammon joint in your slow cooker. Add the onions, oranges, cinnamon, mulled wine, fennel bulb, star anise and peppercorns. Top up with warm water until the gammon is almost covered.
- Cook on low for 8 hours.
- Remove from the slow cooker.
- Preheat the oven to 200°C/gas mark 6.
- Remove the fat from the top of the gammon joint. Score with a knife, then add some cloves to the top of the gammon. Place the gammon in your roasting tray.
- Gently melt the 3 tablespoons of red wine, the orange zest and redcurrant jelly. Brush this over the gammon to form a glaze.
- Bake in the oven for 20–30 minutes, just long enough to brown and crisp the gammon. Serve hot or cold.

Ham, Bean and Vegetable Casserole

Slow cooker or casserole dish

Olive oil (only if cooking on the hob)	300g ham or gammon, in thick chunks
1 onion, finely chopped	120g lean bacon, chopped
2 cloves of garlic, crushed	1 tin haricot beans
2 sweet potatoes, cubed	1 teaspoon paprika
2 carrots, finely sliced	500ml stock
2 sticks of celery, sliced	Seasoning to taste

To cook on the hob
- Heat the oil in a large sauté pan or casserole dish and fry the onion and garlic for 5 minutes. Add the remaining vegetables. Stir gently for 3–4 minutes to help soften the vegetables.
- Add all the remaining ingredients and heat gently. Cook slowly for 1–1½ hours. Stir occasionally and add more liquid if necessary.

To cook in a slow cooker
- Preheat your slow cooker as directed in the manufacturer's instructions.
- Place all the ingredients in the slow cooker. Set the cooker to high and cook for 6 hours or low for 8 hours.
- This can either be liquidised or you can add more stock to make a lovely soup.

Roasted Cherry Tomato, Pancetta and Ricotta Pasta

Saucepan and ovenproof dish

1 small red onion, quartered	1 teaspoon dried thyme
4 cloves garlic, sliced	1 teaspoon dried oregano
½ a red pepper, sliced	300g dried pasta
4–5 rashers of pancetta or lean bacon	125g ricotta
330g cherry tomatoes (one punnet)	1 bunch fresh basil leaves
4 tablespoons olive oil	Seasoning to taste

- Place the onion, garlic, pepper, pancetta or bacon and cherry tomatoes in a roasting dish (one that can also be used to serve from) with the olive oil and dried herbs and mix thoroughly, making sure every item is covered in oil. Cook gently on the hob for 10–15 minutes, turning occasionally.
- Meanwhile, cook the pasta in boiling water according to the instructions on the packet.
- Drain the pasta and add to the roasting dish. Mix thoroughly. Add the ricotta and basil and stir well. Season to taste.
- Garnish with grated parmesan and serve immediately.

Tomato, Paprika and Pork Casserole

Slow cooker or casserole dish

Olive oil

1 red onion, finely chopped

½ a red pepper, sliced

500g pork, cut into chunks

1 tablespoon paprika

1 glass of red wine

1 tin of chopped tomatoes

25g sun-dried tomatoes

100ml stock

100ml crème fraiche

Fresh chopped parsley to garnish

To cook on the hob

- Heat the olive oil in an ovenproof casserole dish or large sauté pan and fry the onion and red pepper until they start to soften.
- Add the pork chunks and cook until brown, before adding the paprika, followed by the wine.
- Add the chopped tomatoes, sun-dried tomatoes and stock. Stir well, before covering with a lid and leaving to simmer on a medium heat for 30 minutes. Add more stock if needed.
- Just prior to serving, add the crème fraiche. Cook for another 2 minutes before serving. Sprinkle with chopped parsley to garnish.

To cook in a slow cooker

- Preheat your slow cooker as directed in the manufacturer's instructions.
- Place all the ingredients apart from the crème fraiche and parsley in the slow cooker. Make sure you warm the stock before adding it as this will maintain the temperature. Turn your cooker to low and cook for 6–8 hours (you can increase the heat to medium if you want this cooked within 4–6 hours). Add more stock if needed.
- Just prior to serving, stir in the crème fraiche and garnish with chopped parsley.

Spaghetti Carbonara

Saucepan

350g spaghetti

Olive oil

2 cloves of garlic, crushed

150g lean bacon, ham or pancetta, chopped

2 eggs

125g Parmesan cheese, grated

Pinch of cayenne pepper

Seasoning

50ml double cream

Fresh herbs to garnish

- Cook the spaghetti in boiling water according to the instructions on the packet.
- Meanwhile, heat the oil in a sauté pan and fry the garlic and bacon.
- While that is cooking, beat the eggs, grated Parmesan cheese and cayenne pepper together. Season well.
- The bacon should now be cooked so add the double cream and leave to one side while you drain the cooked pasta.
- Return the pasta to the large saucepan. Add the egg mixture and the bacon and cream mixture. Stir well and the egg should start to cook with the heat of the spaghetti. After a few minutes it should be ready to serve.
- Garnish with fresh herbs and grated Parmesan.

Sausage and Tomato Casserole

Casserole or ovenproof dish

Olive oil
1 onion, sliced
1–2 cloves of garlic, crushed
1 red pepper, sliced
8 lean pork sausages
100ml red wine

2 teaspoons cornflour (mixed with a little cold water)
4–5 teaspoons paprika
400g tin chopped tomatoes
2–3 teaspoons of sun-dried tomato purée
250ml stock or water
A handful of fresh parsley

- Heat the oil in an ovenproof casserole dish and fry the onion, garlic, pepper and sausages until the onions are translucent.
- Add the wine, cornflour and paprika and stir for another minute before adding all the remaining ingredients, apart from the parsley.
- Cover with a lid and cook on the lowest heat for 25–35 minutes. Add the fresh parsley 5 minutes before serving.

Sausage, Mash and Red Onion Gravy

This is a real winter warmer and delicious when served with creamy mashed potato and seasonal greens.

Casserole or ovenproof dish

8 sausages	300ml hot meat stock
1–2 red onions, sliced	2 teaspoons redcurrant jelly
Olive oil	300ml red wine
1 tablespoon plain flour or cornflour	Seasoning to taste

- Preheat the oven to 190°C/gas mark 5. Put the potatoes on to steam ready to make your mash.
- Place the sausages and onions in an ovenproof dish, drizzle with a little olive oil and bake in the oven for 15 minutes.
- Mix the flour with a little hot stock in a saucepan and stir well over a low heat. Add the redcurrant jelly and continue to add more stock as the gravy thickens.
- Add the wine and season to taste. Continue to cook until the gravy thickens to the desired consistency (about 8–10 minutes).
- Pour over the sausage and onion mixture and bake in the oven for a further 10 minutes. Meanwhile put your green vegetables on to steam. Mash the potatoes when they are ready.
- Serve and enjoy!

Bacon and Mushroom Pasta

Saucepan and sauté pan

300g dried pasta	100ml white wine
Olive oil	A small handful of mixed fresh herbs such as
1 onion, finely chopped	basil, oregano and thyme (or 1–2 teaspoons
1–2 cloves of garlic, crushed	of dry or frozen)
4–5 rashers of lean bacon	2–3 tablespoons crème fraiche
100g button mushrooms	Seasoning to taste

- Cook the pasta in a pan of boiling water according to the instructions on the packet.
- Meanwhile, heat the oil in a large sauté pan and fry the onion and garlic together for a couple of minutes until the onion starts to soften. Add the bacon and cook for a further 5 minutes before adding the mushrooms.
- Add the wine and herbs and stir thoroughly.
- When the pasta is cooked, drain, and return to the empty saucepan. Replace the saucepan on the still-warm hob and add the crème fraiche. Mix well over the remaining heat for 1 minute.
- Season to taste and serve immediately with a garnish of fresh herbs and parmesan cheese.

Liver and Bacon Casserole

If your slow cooker has a sauté facility you can sauté the onions in olive oil – though, to be honest, I have not noticed that this makes any difference to the taste.

Slow cooker

1 onion, sliced

Olive oil (for sautéing)

120g bacon or lardons, roughly chopped

400g liver, roughly chopped

2 carrots, sliced

1 large leek, sliced

3–4 tomatoes, roughly chopped

75g button mushrooms

150ml red wine

500ml meat stock

2–3 teaspoons wholegrain mustard

1 teaspoon paprika

1 bay leaf

1 teaspoon sage

Seasoning to taste

- Preheat your slow cooker as directed in the manufacturer's instructions.
- Place all the ingredients in the slow cooker and stir well to ensure they are evenly distributed. Make sure the stock is warm when you add it as this will maintain the temperature. Cover and turn the cooker to low for 6–8 hours.
- Serve with mashed potato for a real winter warmer.

Toad in the Hole

This is a very filling dish and is useful for using up odds and ends in the fridge. The batter is a simple pancake mix (flour, egg and milk). You can use any variety of sausages, including vegetarian ones, but for meat eaters low fat or good-quality sausages such as organic are a healthy choice as they are less likely to contain dubious ingredients. If you are using plain sausages, why not add some chopped onion and herbs to the batter mix?

Casserole or ovenproof dish

100g plain flour

1 egg

300ml milk

A splash of olive oil

1 onion, chopped

8 lean sausages

A handful of fresh herbs such as thyme,
    oregano, rosemary, or 2 teaspoons of dried

Seasoning to taste

- Preheat the oven to 180°C/gas mark 4.
- Using an electric blender with a balloon whisk, blend the flour, egg and milk together to form a batter. Mix thoroughly and leave to settle.
- Meanwhile place the olive oil, onion and sausages in a deep ovenproof dish and bake in the oven for 10 minutes, turning occasionally.
- Just before the 10 minutes is up, give the batter mix a quick whizz with your balloon whisk, adding the herbs and seasoning before a final whizz.
- Remove the sausages from the oven and immediately pour over the batter, ensuring that all the sausages are covered.
- Return to the oven and cook for 20–30 minutes until golden.
- Serve with onion gravy and steamed vegetables.

Sausage and Puy Lentil Casserole

Casserole or ovenproof dish

A splash of olive oil

8 lean pork sausages

1 red onion, finely chopped

2–3 cloves of garlic, crushed

1 small pack of pancetta

2 large tomatoes, chopped

1 red pepper, sliced

200ml white wine

125g Puy lentils

1–2 teaspoons tomato purée

1 teaspoon dried thyme

500ml stock

Fresh thyme

- Preheat the oven to 180°C/gas mark 4.
- Place the olive oil, sausages, onion, garlic, pancetta, tomatoes and pepper in a casserole dish and bake in the oven until the sausages start to brown.
- Remove from the oven and pour on the wine. Add the Puy lentils, tomato purée, dried thyme and stock. Return to the oven and cook for another 20–30 minutes.
- Sprinkle with fresh thyme, if you have any, before serving.

Pork Stroganoff

Sauté pan

Olive oil	2–3 teaspoons Dijon mustard
1 onion, finely chopped	100ml white wine
2–3 cloves of garlic, crushed	2 teaspoons fresh chopped parsley or
4 pork chops or 500g leftover roast pork	tarragon
300g mushrooms, sliced	100ml stock
2–3 teaspoons paprika	150ml crème fraiche

- Heat the oil in a large sauté pan and fry the onion and garlic for 1 minute. Add the pork and cook for 3–4 minutes, ensuring it is evenly browned.
- Add the mushrooms, paprika and mustard; stir well, before adding the wine. Some of this will evaporate as you continue to cook for a couple of minutes.
- Add the parsley or tarragon and stock and cook on a low heat for 45 minutes.
- Just before serving, remove from the heat and stir in the crème fraiche to form a creamy sauce.
- Serve on a bed of white rice.

Mum's Slow Cook Pork Chops in Cider

Mum kindly passed on this recipe to me. You can use pork chops, loin or medallions of pork.

Slow cooker

Olive oil

4–6 pork chops

4–6 rashers of bacon

1 red onion, finely chopped

2 sticks of celery, sliced

4 potatoes, diced

2–3 carrots, diced

2 parsnips, diced

300ml cider

300ml pork or chicken stock

1 bay leaf

2 teaspoons tarragon

1–2 teaspoons honey

Seasoning to taste

2–3 tablespoons crème fraiche

- If your slow cooker has a sauté facility, or if you can use your pan on the hob, brown the pork in a little olive oil. Alternatively, use a frying pan or sauté pan for this and then transfer the pork to your preheated slow cooker.
- Place the pork in the slow cooker and add all the remaining ingredients, apart from the crème fraiche. Make sure the stock is warm when you add it as this will maintain the temperature.
- Season and cook on high for 4–6 hours, until the vegetables are tender.
- Remove the bay leaf. Just prior to serving, stir in the crème fraiche – this will give a creamy taste and will slightly thicken the sauce if needed.

Chorizo and Home-made Baked Beans

Casserole dish

150g dried haricot beans (or 2 tins of haricot beans)

Olive oil

75g chorizo sausage, sliced

1 onion, chopped

2 cloves of garlic, crushed

75ml apple juice

500g chopped tomatoes

Tomato purée to taste

A generous dash of Worcestershire sauce

1 teaspoon mustard

½ teaspoon cumin

A pinch of chilli powder

Seasoning to taste

- If you are using dried beans, soak them overnight in water. Next day, rinse the beans under cold running water and drain them. Bring to the boil in plenty of water. Boil fast for 10 minutes and then cover and simmer for 40 minutes or until soft. Drain away the water and keep the beans to one side. If using tinned beans, go straight to step 2.
- Heat the olive oil in a casserole dish or sauté pan and fry the sausage, onion and garlic until the onion is soft. Add all the remaining ingredients, including the beans, and simmer on a low heat for 1 hour, stirring occasionally. Season to taste.

One Pot Lamb

Lamb Cutlets in Mushroom Sauce

Sauté pan and grill

25g butter
200g button mushrooms
250ml red wine
1 teaspoon Worcestershire sauce

2 teaspoons paprika
4–8 lamb cutlets
Seasoning to taste

- Melt the butter in a sauté pan and fry the mushrooms until they start to soften.
- Add the wine, Worcestershire sauce and paprika. Cook until the sauce reduces slightly.
- Meanwhile, sprinkle a little paprika over the cutlets and season to taste. Grill for 5 minutes on each side.
- Once cooked, add the cutlets to the sauté pan and cover them with the sauce. Serve immediately.

Slow Cook Lamb and Olive Tagine

Slow cooker

Olive oil

1 large red onion, finely chopped

3 cloves of garlic, crushed

½ a chopped chilli

5cm (2in) knuckle of ginger, chopped

2 teaspoons ground cumin

1 teaspoon ground cinnamon

1 teaspoon ground ginger

1 teaspoon ground coriander

500g lamb stewing meat, cut into chunks

300ml red wine

300ml lamb stock

200g pitted olives

Fresh coriander leaves

Flaked almonds

- Preheat your slow cooker as directed in the manufacturer's instructions.
- If you are using a slow cooker with a sauté option, heat the olive oil on this setting, or you may be able to place the inner pot directly on the hob (refer to the manufacturer's instructions for more details). Alternatively, you can start this in a sauté pan then transfer to your slow cooker.
- Fry the onion, garlic, chilli and ginger in the oil until starting to soften. Add the spices and cook for 1–2 minutes to allow the flavours out.
- Add the meat and brown well in the spices. Transfer to your slow cooker (if necessary) and add all the remaining ingredients apart from the fresh coriander and the almonds. Make sure the stock is warm when you add it as this will maintain the temperature of your cooker.
- Cook on low for 8 hours – the longer the cooking time, the more tender the meat.
- Garnish with a sprinkle of fresh coriander leaves and flaked almonds before serving.

Note: If you don't have a slow cooker, you can cook this in a casserole dish or in a tagine. Cook as above and simmer gently on the hob for 2 hours. Serve with couscous.

Irish Lamb Stew

Slow cooker

1 onion, finely chopped	150g bacon or lardons
2 cloves of garlic, crushed	Sprigs of fresh thyme
2 carrots, thickly sliced	1 bay leaf
2–3 potatoes, thickly diced	200ml white wine
400g lamb	500ml lamb stock

- Preheat the slow cooker as directed in the manufacturer's instructions.
- Chop all the vegetables into chunks.
- Place all the ingredients in the slow cooker. Mix well to ensure they are evenly distributed. Make sure the stock is warm when you add it as this will maintain the temperature.
- Set the slow cooker to low and cook for 6–8 hours, until the lamb is tender.

Slow Cook Lamb and Fennel

Slow cooker

Boneless lamb loin joint

Olive oil

3 cloves of garlic, crushed

2 teaspoons honey

2 teaspoons oregano

1 teaspoon fennel seeds

1 red onion, chopped

2 potatoes, diced

1 sweet potato, diced

2 celery sticks, sliced

1 large carrot, sliced

700g fennel, sliced

600ml lamb stock

200ml white wine

Seasoning to taste

- Place the lamb on a plate. Mix the oil, garlic, honey, oregano and fennel seeds together and rub into the lamb. Cover with cling film or a plastic bag and leave in the fridge overnight.
- The next morning, preheat your slow cooker as directed in the manufacturer's instructions. Prepare the vegetables.
- Place the vegetables and all the remaining ingredients in the slow cooker. Make sure the stock is warm when you add it as this will maintain the temperature. Remove the lamb from the fridge and place in the slow cooker.
- Turn your cooker to high and cook for 6 hours.
- If you would like your lamb to have a crust, remove from the slow cooker when cooked. Turn your conventional oven up to high (200°C/gas mark 6). Place the lamb on a roasting tray and roast for 20 minutes. You could make up and add more of the glaze if needed.
- Serve with the slow cooked vegetables and home-made gravy.

Creamy Lamb Curry

Sauté pan

Olive oil

1 onion, finely chopped

2–3 cloves of garlic, crushed

2.5–5cm (1–2in) piece of ginger, finely chopped

1 chilli, finely chopped

1 teaspoon cumin seeds

400g lamb, diced

½ bunch of spring onions, roughly chopped

1 green pepper, sliced

2–3 teaspoons medium curry powder or paste

½ can of coconut milk (you can freeze the rest)

200ml lamb stock

A small handful of fresh coriander leaves, chopped

- Sauté the onion, garlic, ginger, chilli and cumin seeds in olive oil for 2–3 minutes to help soften.
- Add the lamb and cook for a further 5 minutes before adding the spring onions and pepper slices. Cook for another 5 minutes.
- Add the curry powder/paste, coconut milk and stock and half the coriander leaves. Cover and cook gently for 15 minutes.
- Add the remaining coriander leaves just prior to serving.
- Serve with rice and a selection of breads and chutneys.

Lamb and Apricot Casserole

This is a lovely wholesome dish. You can use lesser cuts of lamb as the long, slow cooking will tenderise the meat. Why not make double the amount and freeze half for another meal?

Casserole, ovenproof dish or slow cooker

Olive oil

1 onion, chopped

2–3 garlic cloves, crushed

400g lamb, diced

3 teaspoons harissa paste or hot chilli paste

2 teaspoons ground cinnamon powder

200ml red wine

1 tin chopped tomatoes

200ml water or stock

1 tin chickpeas

100g chopped apricots

Fresh coriander leaves for garnish

To cook on the hob
- Heat a little oil in a large casserole dish and fry the onion, garlic and lamb for 2–3 minutes.
- Add the harissa paste and stir well for 2 minutes.
- Add all the remaining ingredients and cook slowly on a low heat for 1 hour.
- Garnish with coriander leaves before serving.

To cook in a slow cooker
- Preheat your slow cooker as directed in the manufacturer's instructions.
- Using your slow cooker pan or a sauté pan, heat the oil and fry the onion, garlic and lamb until browned and the onions start to soften. (You can ignore this step if you don't want to brown the meat.)
- Return the onion, garlic and lamb to the slow cooker and add all the remaining ingredients. Make sure the stock is warm when you add it as this will maintain the temperature of the cooker. Cook on high for 6 hours, or low for 8 hours.
- Garnish with coriander leaves before serving.

Lamb Shanks

Slow cooker

2 red onions	300ml red wine
3 cloves of garlic, crushed	3 teaspoons balsamic vinegar
2 sticks of celery, finely sliced	400ml lamb stock
1 leek, finely sliced	1 bay leaf
1 carrot, finely diced	Sprigs of fresh thyme and rosemary
4 lamb shanks	Seasoning to taste
1 tin of chopped tomatoes	

- Preheat your slow cooker as directed in the manufacturer's instructions.
- Prepare all the vegetables. Place all the ingredients in the slow cooker, ensuring that they are combined well and evenly distributed. Make sure the stock is warm when you add it as this will maintain the temperature.
- Set the slow cooker to low and cook for 6–8 hours, until the lamb is tender. Prior to serving, if your liquid is too thin, stir in 1–2 teaspoons of cornflour, dissolved in a little water. Turn up the heat for 5–10 minutes to thicken it.
- Season to taste before serving.

Lamb, Butter Bean and Tomato Casserole

This is a perfect slow cook dish for cheaper cuts of lamb, as the longer you cook it, the tenderer the meat will be.

Slow cooker

1 onion, finely chopped

2 sticks of celery, sliced

1 red pepper, finely sliced

1 large carrot, diced

450g stewing lamb, diced

1 punnet of cherry tomatoes

1 x 400g tin of butter beans

500ml lamb stock

2 teaspoons sun-dried tomato paste

1 teaspoon oregano

Seasoning to taste

- Preheat your slow cooker as directed in the manufacturer's instructions.
- Add all the ingredients to the slow cooker and set to low. Make sure the stock is warm when you add it as this will maintain the temperature. Mix the ingredients so they are evenly distributed.
- Cook for 6–8 hours. Season to taste before serving.

Lamb and Almond Tagine

This is a lovely rich recipe. You can cheat by adding a spicy tagine sauce instead of the individual spices. I have used Al'Fez Honey and Almond Tagine Sauce (£1.99 a jar) which has a very authentic flavour and is great for when you are in a hurry. For more information visit www.alfez.com

Casserole, ovenproof dish or slow cooker

Olive oil	I carrot
I large onion, chopped	8 shallots
2–3 cloves of garlic, crushed	I sweet potato
I teaspoon coriander seeds	I tablespoon honey
I teaspoon cumin seeds	600ml water or stock
2 teaspoons chilli powder	I glass of red wine
3–4 teaspoons paprika	50g almond flakes
3–4 teaspoons turmeric	Seasoning to taste
3–4 teaspoons cinnamon powder	Chopped fresh coriander to garnish
400g lamb, diced	

To cook on the hob
- Heat the oil in a large ovenproof dish and sauté the onion and garlic.
- Add the herbs, spices and lamb. Continue to cook for 2–3 minutes.
- Add the carrot, shallots and sweet potato and sweat for another minute or two before adding the remaining ingredients.
- Cook slowly on a low heat for 1 hour. If you are using one of the cheaper cuts of lamb, cook on a very low heat for longer as this will help tenderise the meat.
- Stir occasionally and add more liquid if necessary as this may evaporate as you cook.
- Sprinkle with a few more almond flakes and chopped fresh coriander before serving with couscous or rice.

To cook in a slow cooker
- Preheat your slow cooker as directed in the manufacturer's instructions.
- Sauté the onions and garlic in a little olive oil. If you don't have a sauté facility in your slow cooker, use a sauté or frying pan for this.
- Add the herbs, spices and lamb. Continue to cook for 2–3 minutes.

- Transfer (if applicable) to your slow cooker and add all the remaining ingredients. Make sure the stock is warm when you add it as this will maintain the temperature. Cover and cook gently on low for 6–8 hours.
- Sprinkle with a few more almond flakes and chopped fresh coriander before serving with couscous or rice.

Lamb and Green Lentil Curry

The green lentils help bulk out the curry so you don't need to use as much lamb. I have made this with a medium curry powder, but you can opt for hot or mild depending on your personal taste.

Sauté pan

Olive oil	1 tablespoon medium curry powder
1 onion, sliced	Juice of ½ a lemon
2–3 cloves of garlic, crushed	1 tin of chopped tomatoes
2.5cm (1in) knuckle of fresh ginger, sliced	150g green lentils
400g lamb, cut into chunks	500ml water or lamb stock
1–2 chillies, finely cut	A small handful of chopped fresh coriander
1 teaspoon cinnamon powder	150g low fat yoghurt or quark

- Heat the oil in a pan and fry the onion, garlic and ginger for 1 minute.
- Add the lamb, chillies, cinnamon and curry powder and stir well for 3–4 minutes.
- Add the lemon juice, tomatoes, lentils and stock and half the coriander. Cover with a lid and cook for 1 hour until the lamb is tender.
- Just prior to serving, stir in the yoghurt and remaining coriander.

Lamb Hotpot

A traditional winter warmer, this makes a nourishing and sustaining family meal.

Sauté pan and casserole or ovenproof dish

400g lamb, cubed	Knob of butter
50g plain flour	500ml lamb stock
2–3 teaspoons paprika	2–3 sprigs of thyme (or a cube of frozen fresh thyme)
Olive oil	
3–4 leeks, sliced	I teaspoon mixed herbs
2 cloves of garlic, crushed	6–8 potatoes, thinly sliced
1–2 carrots, chopped	25g mature Cheddar, grated

- Preheat the oven to 180°C/gas mark 4.
- Place the lamb in a bowl and mix with the flour and paprika, ensuring the lamb is evenly coated with flour all over.
- Heat the oil in a large sauté pan and fry the leeks and garlic for 2–3 minutes. Add the meat, carrots and butter and cook for a further 2–3 minutes to help brown the meat.
- Pour on the stock and herbs and cook for 10 minutes.
- Arrange a layer of potato slices in the bottom of your ovenproof dish. Add a layer of the meat mixture and continue to alternate, finishing with a final layer of potato slices.
- Bake in the oven for 1 hour
- Remove from the oven and sprinkle the grated cheese over the top before returning the hotpot to the oven for a final 20–30 minutes.

Lamb Moussaka

Sauté pan and ovenproof dish

2–3 aubergines, sliced
Olive oil
1 onion, sliced
2 cloves of garlic, crushed
400g lamb mince
1 tin of chopped tomatoes
2 teaspoons tomato purée

1 teaspoon dried mint
2 teaspoons cinnamon powder
Seasoning to taste
300ml low fat crème fraiche
50g mature Cheddar or Parmesan cheese,
  grated

- Add the aubergine slices to a pan of boiling water for 2 minutes. Remove and pat dry. Leave to one side.
- Meanwhile, heat a little olive oil in a sauté pan and fry the onion and garlic. Add the lamb and cook until brown.
- Add the tomatoes and purée, mint and cinnamon and cook for another 2–3 minutes. Season to taste.
- Place a layer of mince in an ovenproof dish, followed by a layer of aubergine. Finish with a layer of mince.
- Mix the crème fraiche with the grated cheese and pour over the final layer of mince. Garnish with a sprinkle of Parmesan before baking in the oven for 30–40 minutes.

Shepherd's Pie

Sauté pan, steamer and ovenproof dish

800g potatoes, cut into rough chunks

4 carrots, 2 cut into small cubes, 2 roughly chopped

1 onion, chopped

400g lean minced lamb (or drained of fat)

75g mushrooms, sliced (optional)

100ml red wine

1 teaspoon yeast extract (Marmite or similar)

200ml meat gravy (or vegetable gravy if using veggie mince)

Seasoning to taste

Worcestershire sauce

25g butter

75g mature Cheddar, grated

A sprinkle of paprika

- Preheat the oven to 180°C/gas mark 4.
- Place the potatoes and the 2 roughly chopped carrots in a steamer and cook until soft.
- Meanwhile, in a large sauté pan, fry the onion for 1–2 minutes before adding the mince.
- Cook until the mince is brown before adding the 2 cubed carrots, the mushrooms and wine.
- Dissolve the yeast extract in the hot gravy before adding to the mince. Cook for 20 minutes until the meat and vegetables are tender and the gravy is reduced to the desired consistency. Season to taste and add the Worcestershire sauce.
- Mash the potatoes and carrots together. Add the butter and two thirds of the Cheddar. Mix thoroughly.
- Place the mince in a deep baking dish and spoon mash over the top. Be careful not to overfill the dish. Press down gently with a fork. Top with the remaining grated cheese and a sprinkle of paprika.
- Bake in the oven for 30 minutes.

Lamb, Shallot and Mushroom Casserole

Slow cooker

250g shallots or baby onions	200ml red wine
2 cloves of garlic, crushed	300ml lamb stock
500g lamb, cut into chunks	I teaspoon paprika
200g button mushrooms	Sprigs of fresh rosemary
I tin chopped tomatoes	Seasoning to taste
2 teaspoons tomato purée	

- Preheat your slow cooker as directed in the manufacturer's instructions.
- Prepare all the vegetables. Place all the ingredients in the slow cooker, ensuring they are combined well and evenly distributed. Make sure the stock is warm when you add it as this will maintain the temperature.
- Set the slow cooker to low and cook for 6–8 hours, until the lamb is tender.

Slow Cook Leg of Lamb

This is a really simple dish and makes moist, tender lamb. You can coat the lamb with whatever herbs and spices you wish. If you are not sure if a leg of lamb will fit in your slow cooker, ask your butcher to saw off the end of the bone. Alternatively, buy one without the bone.

Slow cooker

Leg of lamb	Salt
3–5 cloves of garlic	Black pepper
1 teaspoon rosemary	1 tablespoon of honey
Juice of 1 lemon	225ml red wine

- Combine the garlic, rosemary, lemon, salt, pepper and honey together to form a paste. Rub this into the leg of lamb. Cover and leave in the fridge overnight.
- Preheat your slow cooker as directed in the manufacturer's instructions.
- Place the lamb in the slow cooker. Pour the wine around the sides of the lamb.
- Set your slow cooker to low and cook for 8 hours.
- If you would like a crisp coating, melt 50g of butter with 2–3 tablespoons of maple syrup in a saucepan. Remove the leg of lamb from the slow cooker when cooked. Transfer it to a roasting tin, coat with the butter syrup and place in a hot oven (200°C/gas mark 6) for 15–20 minutes.

One Pot Roast Lamb Chops and Vegetables

This is a very simple dish. Just prepare the vegetables and add it all to your roasting pan.

Roasting pan

Olive oil

3 red onions cut into quarters

2 large potatoes cut into wedges

2–3 cloves of garlic, finely chopped

2 sweet potatoes cut into wedges

1 parsnip, cut into thin lengths

2 carrots cut into lengths

4–5 sprigs of rosemary

2–3 teaspoons paprika

4–6 lamb chops

100ml hot lamb stock

50ml red wine (or you can use another 50ml
of stock if you prefer)

Seasoning to taste

- Preheat the oven to 200°C/gas mark 6.
- Cut the vegetables into the required lengths. I keep the skins on the potatoes, but it is personal choice. Place the vegetables in a bowl. Add a generous glug of olive oil. Ensure all the vegetables are well coated in oil.
- Pour the vegetables into a roasting tin. Sprinkle with rosemary and paprika. Bake in the oven for 20 minutes.
- Rub some oil into the lamb chops and sprinkle them with more paprika. Remove the vegetables from the oven after 20 minutes and add the chops to the roasting pan with the vegetables.
- Cook for another 20 minutes, until the vegetables and chops are tender. Mix the hot lamb stock and the wine together. Pour over the vegetable and chop mix and return everything to the oven for 5 minutes.
- Season and serve.

Spicy Shepherd's Pie with Sweet Potato Topping

This is a great variation on the traditional shepherd's pie. I love the sweet potato topping.

Sauté pan, steamer and ovenproof dish

800g sweet potatoes cut into rough chunks

4 carrots, 2 cut into small cubes, 2 roughly chopped

1 onion, chopped

2 cloves of garlic, crushed

1 pepper, finely chopped

1 chilli, finely chopped (optional)

400g lean minced lamb (or drained of fat)

1–2 teaspoons chilli powder (to taste)

½ teaspoon coriander

½ teaspoon cumin

2–3 tomatoes, chopped

200ml meat stock

100ml red wine

Seasoning to taste

25g butter

25g mature Cheddar, grated

Paprika

- Preheat the oven to 180°C/gas mark 4.
- Place the potatoes and the 2 roughly chopped carrots in a steamer and cook until soft.
- Meanwhile, in a large sauté pan, fry the onion, garlic, pepper and chilli for 1–2 minutes before adding the mince. Add all the remaining spices.
- Cook until the mince is brown before adding the 2 cubed carrots, the tomatoes, stock and wine.
- Cook for 20 minutes until the meat and vegetables are tender and the gravy is reduced to the desired consistency. Season to taste.
- Mash the potatoes and carrots together. Add the butter and mix thoroughly.
- Place the mince in a deep baking dish and spoon mash on top. Be careful not to overfill the dish. Press down gently with a fork. Top with grated cheese and a sprinkle of paprika.
- Bake in the oven for 30 minutes.

Lamb, Tomato and Haricot Bean Casserole

Slow cooker

500g stewing lamb, cut into chunks

1 large onion, finely chopped

2 cloves of garlic, crushed

2 carrots, sliced

2 sticks of celery, sliced

1 parsnip, sliced

1 tin of chopped tomatoes

1 tin of haricot beans

2–3 teaspoons sun-dried tomato purée

500ml lamb or vegetable stock

1 bouquet garni

1 teaspoon dried parsley

Seasoning to taste

- Preheat your slow cooker as directed in the manufacturer's instructions.
- There is no need to brown the meat; it makes no difference to the flavour. Simply add all the ingredients to the slow cooker,, ensuring they are evenly distributed.
- Turn your slow cooker to low and cook for 6–8 hours.

Lancashire Hotpot

Slow cooker

400g lamb, cut into chunks

2 lambs' kidneys, diced

150ml red wine (optional)

2 teaspoons of thyme

300ml lamb stock (or 400ml if not using wine)

2 onions, finely chopped

125g mushrooms, quartered

500g potatoes, sliced

Seasoning to taste

- Preheat your slow cooker as directed in the manufacturer's instructions.
- There is no need to brown the meat unless you prefer to do so; it makes no difference to the flavour. Mix the wine, thyme and stock together.
- Place the meat, onions and mushrooms, scattered with thyme, in the base of your slow cooker. Pour half the stock mix over the meat. Make sure the stock is warm when you add it as this will maintain the temperature of your cooker. Follow this with the slices of potato and season to taste.
- Pour the remaining stock over the hotpot.
- Turn your slow cooker to medium or high and cook for 4–6 hours.

One Pot Fish

Tuna Bitza Salad

Excuse the name but this really is great for using up any spare ingredients in your fridge to make bits of this and bits of that salad.

Serving bowl

A selection of leaf lettuce

1 tin of tuna, cut into chunks

½ a bunch of spring onions, sliced

½ a pepper, thinly sliced

4–5 mangetout or sugar snap peas, roughly chopped

4 eggs, boiled and halved

A handful of fresh chives and mint, combined

For the dressing

50ml olive oil or omega-rich oil

Juice of ½ a lemon

Seasoning to taste

- Arrange the lettuce leaves in the base of a large serving bowl. Add the tuna, spring onions, pepper and mangetout/sugar snap peas.
- Place the boiled egg halves over the lettuce leaves. Sprinkle with freshly chopped herbs.
- To make a dressing, mix the oil, lemon juice and seasoning together. Drizzle over the salad just before serving.

Note: You can add just about any leftover item in your fridge: cold meat, chopped tomatoes or even chunks of feta cheese. Experiment and make something out of nothing!

Quick and Easy Prawn Rice

Large sauté pan with lid

Olive oil

1 red onion, finely chopped

2 cloves of garlic, finely chopped

½–1 chilli, depending on taste

2–3 tablespoons curry paste (to taste)

300g basmati rice

700ml fish stock

1 teaspoon turmeric

3–4 spring onions, finely chopped, including stalks

150g pack of cooked prawns (if frozen, these should be defrosted)

50g peas (if frozen, these should be defrosted)

50g sweetcorn

1 red pepper, finely diced

Fresh chopped parsley or coriander leaves

1 lemon, cut into wedges

- Heat the oil in a large sauté pan and fry the onion, garlic and chilli until the onion starts to soften.
- Add the curry paste, and then the rice, ensuring it is thoroughly coated in the paste.
- Add the stock and turmeric. Cover and cook on medium heat for 10 minutes.
- Add the spring onions, prawns, peas, sweetcorn and pepper. Remove from the heat and keep covered for another 8–10 minutes.
- Fluff up with a fork, add the chopped herbs and serve immediately with lemon wedges.

Coley Cobbler

Saucepan and ovenproof dish

For the fish casserole
400g coley
50g butter
100g prawns
½ a bunch of spring onions, finely chopped
1 tablespoon plain flour
350–500ml milk
1–2 teaspoons wholegrain mustard
Seasoning to taste

½ a teaspoon dried parsley
75g cheese, grated
1 small can of sweetcorn

For the cobbler topping
30g butter
150g self-raising flour
125ml milk

- Preheat the oven to 200°C/gas mark 6.
- Cut the fish into chunks, removing the bones and skin. Dip into a small amount of flour ensuring it is evenly coated.
- Melt the butter in a large sauté pan and fry the fish, prawns and spring onions for 3–4 minutes.
- Place in an ovenproof dish, retaining the butter in the sauté pan (if this has dried up, you may need to add some more.)
- Add the plain flour to the melted butter and stir well. Gradually add the milk, stirring continuously to make a white sauce. I normally use a whisk. When you are happy with the consistency and thickness of the sauce, you can start to flavour it.
- Add the mustard, seasoning, parsley and cheese. Stir well until the cheese has melted. Drain the sweetcorn and stir into the sauce.
- Pour onto the fish and stir well ensuring the fish is evenly coated in sauce.

To make the cobbler topping
- Rub the butter into the self-raising flour to form breadcrumbs. Gradually add the cold milk (you may not need all of this), until you form a dough
- On a floured board, gently knead the dough and roll to 2cm thickness. Cut into round scones. Arrange the scones over the top of the fish dish, either around the edges or to cover the top completely.
- Brush the scones with milk before baking in the oven for 30 minutes, until the scones are risen and brown.

Kedgeree

This is traditionally a breakfast dish, but there is no reason you can't have it at any time of day. To make this quick and easy, plan ahead. Cook the eggs and, if you have a rice dish the night before, keep some cooked rice aside for the kedgeree.

Saucepan

150g long-grain rice	2 teaspoons curry powder
125ml milk	3 spring onions, finely chopped
400g boneless haddock	Juice and zest of ½ a lemon
3 hard-boiled eggs	A handful of fresh parsley, finely chopped
A pinch of cayenne pepper	Seasoning to taste

- Cook the rice in a saucepan until tender.
- Bring the milk to the boil in a saucepan and add the haddock. Cook for 4–5 minutes. Drain away the liquid. Cut the haddock into chunks.
- Hard-boil the eggs and chop them into chunks.
- Drain the rice. Stir in the spices, haddock, spring onions, hard-boiled eggs, lemon zest and juice and parsley. Season to taste. Stir well and serve immediately.

Tuna and Chilli Linguine

Saucepan and casserole dish

300g linguine

Olive oil

½ a bunch of spring onions, finely chopped, including green stalks

2 cloves of garlic, crushed

1 red chilli, finely chopped

350ml white wine

350g tuna, in chunks

75g rocket

50g cherry tomatoes, halved

Parmesan cheese

- Cook the linguine according to the instructions on the packet.
- Meanwhile, heat the olive oil in a large casserole dish (you will be using this to serve the whole meal in so make sure it is an adequate size) and fry the spring onions, garlic and chilli until soft. Add the wine and cook for 2–3 minutes, allowing it to reduce slightly.
- Add the tuna chunks and stir well. Turn off the heat.
- Meanwhile, drain the pasta and add to the tuna mix.
- Add the rocket, cherry tomatoes and a sprinkle of Parmesan. Stir well and serve immediately.

Prawn and Scallop Paella

Sauté pan

Olive oil

1 red onion, finely chopped

2 cloves of garlic, crushed

1 red pepper, finely chopped

250g paella or risotto rice

200ml white wine

800ml fish stock

1 teaspoon turmeric

1 bay leaf

100g frozen peas

50g sweetcorn

250g scallops

250g large prawns

A handful of chopped parsley

3–4 lemons, quartered

- Heat the olive oil in a large sauté pan (it should be big enough to fit the entire meal in it – make sure it has a lid!) and fry the onion, garlic and red pepper for 3–4 minutes to help soften.
- Add the rice and stir thoroughly ensuring it is coated with the oil and juices from the onion and garlic. Add the wine and cook for 2–3 minutes before adding the fish stock.
- Add the turmeric and bay leaf, cover and cook the rice for 10 minutes.
- Add the peas, sweetcorn, scallops and prawns and continue until they are thoroughly cooked and the stock is absorbed. Remove the bay leaf before stirring in the chopped parsley.
- Serve with lemon wedges and a garnish of chopped herbs or parsley.

Sweetcorn and Tuna Pasta

Saucepan and sauté pan

300g dried pasta
10ml olive oil
1 onion, finely chopped
1 tin tuna, drained

1 small tin of sweetcorn or 125g frozen
   sweetcorn, defrosted
200ml milk
200g low fat cream cheese
Seasoning to taste

- Cook the pasta in a pan of boiling water according to the instructions on the packet.
- Meanwhile, fry the onion in olive oil until soft. Add the tuna and sweetcorn and stir well. Turn off the heat. Add the milk and cream cheese and cover the pan with a lid to keep warm. Everything will start to melt together.
- Drain the pasta and return to the empty saucepan. Add the tuna mix. Mix well over the heat of the still-warm hob for 1 minute.
- Season to taste and sprinkle with some fresh herbs if you have any.
- Serve immediately.

Creamy Fish Pie

Saucepan and ovenproof dish

1kg potatoes
500g fish fillets (or ask your fishmonger for
   bits of flaky white fish)
200g salmon pieces (optional)
100g prawns (optional)
250ml milk

25g butter
25g flour
1 teaspoon mustard
Seasoning to taste
Grated cheese for topping

- Preheat the oven to 180°C/gas mark 4.
- Boil or steam the potatoes until tender. Once cooked, mash ready for use.
- Meanwhile place the fish and milk in a pan and bring to the boil. Cook for 10 minutes or until the fish is cooked through.
- Drain the fish and retain the liquid for making the creamy sauce.
- Shred the fish ready for use and arrange in your pie dish.
- Melt the butter in a pan and add the flour. Stir in the milk stock and thicken. Add the mustard, season and stir well. Pour over the fish.
- Cover with mashed potato, with a final topping of grated cheese.
- Bake in the oven for 30 minutes.

Macaroni Cheese and Haddock

This is a really simple dish, perfect for a quick supper.

Saucepan and ovenproof dish

500ml milk	50g butter
1 bay leaf	50g plain flour
350g haddock (you can use smoked if you prefer)	Seasoning to taste
	100g mature Cheddar, grated
130g dried macaroni	50g breadcrumbs

- Preheat the oven to 180°C/gas mark 4.
- In a pan, heat the milk to just below boiling point. Add the bay leaf and the filleted haddock chunks. Cook for 3–4 minutes. Remove the haddock and place to one side. Pour the warm milk into a jug.
- Cook the macaroni according to the instructions on the packet.
- Meanwhile, in the pan you cooked the milk in, heat the butter on a low/medium heat until melted. Stir in the flour to form a paste then gradually add the warm milk, stirring continuously. I normally switch to a hand whisk at this point.
- Continue to add the milk and whisk until the sauce starts to thicken. Season and add two thirds of the grated cheese, retaining some for the topping. Make sure your sauce is not really thick at this point as the macaroni and oven heat will thicken it further.
- By this time your macaroni should be almost ready. Drain and mix together the sauce, fish and macaroni and place in an ovenproof dish.
- Top with breadcrumbs and cover with the remaining grated cheese.
- Bake in the oven for 20 minutes until golden brown.

Creamy Thai Fish

This is a really easy dish to prepare, and can be made in a matter of minutes. You can buy Thai kits from supermarkets containing lemon grass, ginger, galangals and garlic. You can also buy fish and seafood pieces in 500g packs from supermarkets – ideal for this type of dish or a fish pie.

Wok or sauté pan

2 chillies

2.5cm (1in) knuckle of ginger

1 teaspoon Thai paste

1–2 teaspoons Thai fish sauce

A small handful of fresh coriander

1–2 sticks of lemon grass

300ml low fat coconut milk

Olive oil

1 red onion, chopped

2 cloves of garlic, crushed

500g pack of seafood pieces

- Place the chilli, ginger, Thai paste, fish sauce, coriander, lemon grass and coconut milk in a blender and whizz until smooth. Leave to one side.
- Meanwhile, heat the oil in a wok or sauté pan and cook the onion and garlic until the onion starts to soften. Add the fish/seafood pieces and cook for 3–4 minutes until cooked.
- Pour the sauce over the fish and onion and heat for 3–4 minutes. Remove from the heat and serve.

Fish Stew

Casserole dish

Olive oil	300ml white wine
I onion, finely chopped	520g fish fillets or pieces
2 cloves of garlic, crushed	12 prawns
I red pepper, deseeded and diced	2 bay leaves
I tin of chopped tomatoes, or 6 ripe tomatoes	A handful of fresh parsley, chopped
300ml fish stock	Seasoning to taste

- Heat the oil in a casserole dish and fry the onion, garlic and pepper for 2–3 minutes to help soften.
- Add all the remaining ingredients, cover and cook on a medium heat for 30–40 minutes.
- Season to taste before serving.

Fish Biryani

Saucepan and sauté pan

For the rice

Olive oil

4 cloves

4 peppercorns

1 cinnamon stick

4 green cardamoms

3–4 spring onions

350g basmati rice

2 bay leaves

For the fish dish

Olive oil

1 small onion, finely chopped

2–3 cloves of garlic, crushed

1–2 chillies, finely chopped

1–2 teaspoons grated ginger

1 teaspoon cumin seeds

2 teaspoons garam masala

1 tablespoon coriander powder

1 teaspoon chilli powder

1 teaspoon turmeric powder

400g fish pieces or fillets, cubed

3–4 tablespoons yoghurt

Freshly chopped coriander to garnish

- Place all the rice ingredients, except the rice and bay leaves, in a deep pan and cook for 2 minutes. Add the rice and stir well.
- Pour over 600ml of water, bring to the boil and cook for no more than 5 minutes.
- Cover the pan with a lid and leave to one side.
- Meanwhile, heat the oil in a pan and fry the onion, garlic, chilli and ginger for 2–3 minutes before adding the spices and the fish.
- Cook until the fish is done – this should take approximately 6–7 minutes.
- Add the yoghurt and stir well.
- Combine the rice and fish dish together before serving. Garnish with freshly chopped coriander.

Fish Crumble

Saucepan and casserole dish

500g fish fillets (or ask your fishmonger for
  bits of flaky white fish)
200g salmon pieces (optional)
100g prawns (optional)
250ml milk
25g butter
25g flour
1 teaspoon mustard
Seasoning to taste

For the crumble topping
75g flour
25g oats
45g butter
1–2 teaspoons parsley
30g mature cheese, grated

- Preheat the oven to 180°C/gas mark 4.
- Place the fish and milk in a pan and bring to the boil. Cook for 10 minutes or until the fish is cooked through.
- Drain the fish and retain the liquid for making the creamy sauce.
- Shred the fish ready for use and place in your pie dish.
- Melt the butter in a pan and add the flour. Stir in the milk stock and thicken.
- Add the mustard, season and stir well. Pour over the fish.
- Combine the flour and oats. Rub in the butter until the mixture resembles breadcrumbs. Add the parsley and grated cheese. Sprinkle over the fish base.
- Bake in the oven for 30 minutes.

Oven-baked Haddock

Roasting or ovenproof dish

Olive oil	12–15 cherry tomatoes
4–6 haddock fillets	A handful of capers
1 red onion, sliced	Sprigs of fresh thyme and rosemary
2 red peppers, sliced	Zest and juice of 1 lemon

- Preheat the oven to 180°C/gas mark 4.
- Sprinkle some olive oil over the base of the roasting or ovenproof dish. Add the fillets of haddock.
- Layer the onion, peppers, tomatoes, capers and herbs over the fillets, with a drizzle of olive oil and the juice and zest of the lemon
- Cover with a lid or tin foil and bake for 20–30 minutes, until the fillets are cooked.

Prawn Curry

Sauté pan

Olive oil	1 teaspoon ground cumin
1 onion, finely chopped	1 teaspoon ground coriander
1–2 cloves of garlic, crushed	500g prawns
1 red pepper, finely chopped	100ml low fat coconut milk
½ a chilli, finely chopped	2–3 tablespoons low fat crème fraiche
1–2 teaspoons Thai curry paste	Fresh coriander, finely chopped

- Heat the oil in a sauté pan and fry the onion and garlic until the onion starts to soften.
- Add the pepper and chilli and cook for another couple of minutes before adding the Thai paste, cumin and coriander. Allow the flavours to be released for a minute or two.
- Add the prawns and fry for 3–4 minutes until they are cooked. Turn down the heat to low.
- Add the coconut milk and crème fraiche (crème fraiche helps to thicken the sauce if necessary, or you can use more coconut milk if you prefer a thinner sauce). Add the chopped coriander leaves. Stir well. Once thoroughly heated, serve on a bed of rice.

Prawn and Asparagus Pasta

Saucepan and sauté pan

300g penne pasta

200g asparagus spears

75g frozen peas

Olive oil

1–2 cloves garlic, crushed

200g prawns

200g low fat crème fraiche

Zest and juice of ½ a lemon

Black pepper

- Cook the pasta in boiling water as directed on the packet. About 4–5 minutes before it is ready, add the asparagus spears and frozen peas.
- Meanwhile, heat the oil in a pan and fry the garlic and prawns until the prawns are transparent. Add the crème fraiche and lemon juice and zest. Season with black pepper.
- Drain the pasta and return to the saucepan. Add the prawn mixture and stir well on a low heat before serving.
- Garnish with fresh chopped herbs or parmesan cheese.

Baked Trout with Roasted Vegetables

Roasting tin or ovenproof dish

4 trout fillets

Olive oil

2–3 cloves of garlic, crushed

1 red chilli, finely chopped

1–2 red peppers, finely sliced into rings

Juice of 1 lemon

Seasoning to taste

1kg new potatoes

1–2 leeks, thickly sliced

1–2 carrots, thickly sliced

1–2 sweet potatoes, cut into thick cubes

2–3 teaspoons paprika

- Preheat the oven to 180°C/gas mark 4.
- Place the fillets or whole trout onto a large, greased piece of tinfoil. Brush the fillets with olive oil. Sprinkle evenly over the fillets, the garlic, chilli and sliced peppers. Squeeze fresh lemon juice over the fish and season well. Seal the foil into a parcel and leave to rest.
- Meanwhile, place the remaining vegetables in a bowl, add 2–3 tablespoons of olive oil and sprinkle on the paprika. Mix well ensuring all the vegetables are thoroughly coated.
- Pour the vegetables into a large ovenproof dish or roasting tin and bake in the oven for 30 minutes.
- Add the foil parcel to the roasting tin and bake for an additional 15–20 minutes, until the fish is tender and flakes when pressed with a fork. Whole trout will take longer to cook.
- Remove the foil and return the fish to the tin before serving.

Leftover Fish Tagine

This is a great recipe for using up any unwanted vegetables hiding in your fridge, as well as any leftover cooked potatoes. In fact, if you think ahead and double up the potatoes for the previous night's dinner, you'll have a really quick and easy meal.

Sauté pan or casserole dish

Olive oil

1 small red onion, finely sliced

2 cloves of garlic, crushed

2 peppers, sliced

2 sticks of celery, chopped

2 teaspoons ground cumin

1 teaspoon ground coriander

1 teaspoon ground cinnamon

1 tin of tomatoes (or 4–6 ripe tomatoes)

150–200ml fish stock

4 cod fillets

4–5 cooked potatoes, cut into chunks or
thickly sliced

1 preserved lemon, chopped

Fresh coriander leaves, chopped

- Gently heat the olive oil in the base of the pan and fry the onion, garlic, peppers and celery for 3–4 minutes.
- Add the ground cumin, coriander and cinnamon and cook for 2 more minutes.
- Add the tomatoes, fish stock, fish fillets, cooked potatoes, chopped preserved lemon and half the chopped coriander. Cover and cook gently for 15–20 minutes.
- Sprinkle with the remaining coriander before serving.

Mediterranean Fish Pot

This is a very simple dish. You can use any white fish, either fillets or speak to your fishmonger as they can give you fish pieces which are often cheaper. You can cook this in a slow cooker, on a low heat in a saucepan or in the oven.

Casserole dish or slow cooker

Olive oil	1 tin of chopped tomatoes
2–3 cloves of garlic, chopped	2 teaspoons basil (I use one frozen cube if I
1 red onion, finely chopped	don't have any fresh)
2 sticks of celery, chopped	2 teaspoons oregano
500g white fish (fillets or pieces)	Juice of 1 lemon
30g sun-dried tomatoes	1 glass of red wine

To cook on the hob
• Heat the oil and fry the garlic and onion. Cook until translucent before adding the celery.
• Add all the remaining ingredients. Cover and cook on a very low heat for 1 hour.
• Serve with new potatoes and green vegetables.

To cook in a slow cooker
• Preheat your slow cooker if necessary according to the manufacturer's instructions.
• Add all the ingredients into the slow cooker (except the olive oil which isn't needed and the fresh herbs) and cook on high for 4–6 hours.
• Add the fresh herbs 30 minutes before serving.
• Serve with new potatoes and green vegetables.

Haddock Risotto

Saucepan or casserole dish

50g butter

1 onion, finely chopped

1 clove of garlic, crushed

300g risotto rice

200ml white wine

75g peas, defrosted if frozen

500–700ml fish stock

200g haddock, skinned, boned and chopped

2–3 tablespoons fresh dill, chopped (you can use frozen but add this to the hot stock before adding to the rice)

- Melt the butter in a saucepan and fry the onion and garlic until translucent.
- Add the rice and stir well, ensuring that the rice is completely covered in the butter mixture. Don't let this stick! If necessary turn the heat down to medium.
- Add the wine and peas and stir thoroughly. The wine will evaporate but will flavour the rice.
- Add the stock (ideally warm or hot stock) a little at a time. Wait until each addition of stock has been absorbed before adding more.
- After 10 minutes, add the chopped haddock and dill and your final spoonful of stock. Stir well until the stock is almost absorbed (the rice will get to a point where it cannot absorb any more liquid).
- Cover the pan with a lid and remove from the heat for 5 minutes.
- Serve immediately.

Cod and Vegetable Casserole

Casserole dish

Olive oil

1 red onion

2 cloves of garlic, crushed

1 red pepper, sliced

1 courgette, sliced

2 sticks of celery, sliced

75g French beans

1 tin of tomatoes

500ml fish stock

1 teaspoon paprika

1 teaspoon dried tarragon

3–4 cod fillets, roughly chopped

Freshly chopped parsley

Seasoning to taste

- Heat the oil in a casserole dish and fry the onion and garlic for 2–3 minutes before adding all the remaining fresh vegetables. Cook for a further 5 minutes.
- Add the tomatoes, stock, paprika and tarragon. Cover and cook for 10 minutes on a medium heat.
- Add the fish and half the chopped parsley. Cover again and cook for 15 minutes.
- Season to taste before serving garnished with the remainder of the parsley.

Slow Cook Sole Parcels

This is a really simple dish – just wrap your fish and chosen ingredients in foil parcels, place in the slow cooker on low and cook for 2–3 hours. You can experiment with many flavours, such as lemon and ginger, or just opt for the flavour of pesto.

Slow cooker

1 red onion	2 tomatoes
1–2 garlic cloves	2 tablespoons red pesto
½ a red pepper	4 sole fillets

- In a blender or attachment for finely chopping, combine the onion, garlic, pepper, tomatoes and red pesto.
- Cut the fillets in half. Take 8 squares of aluminium foil and butter the inner sides.
- Place half a fillet on each square and top with a spoonful of the pesto mix. Fold over the aluminium foil to seal each piece of fish in a parcel.
- Turn the slow cooker to low. Place the parcels in the slow cooker (no need to add water unless you use a crockery pot). Cook for 2–3 hours, until the fillets flake off the fork.
- Serve with new potatoes and green beans.

One Pot Veggie Dishes

Sun-dried Tomato, Pepper and Goats' Cheese Frittata

Ovenproof sauté or frying pan

Olive oil or butter

1 small red onion, finely sliced

1–2 red peppers, finely sliced

4 eggs

1 teaspoon oregano

Seasoning to taste

8–12 sun-dried tomatoes

50g goats' cheese, crumbled

4 tablespoons crème fraiche

- Preheat the oven to 180°C/gas mark 4.
- Melt the butter or oil in a pan and fry the onion and pepper until soft.
- Meanwhile, beat the eggs together, add the herbs and season to taste. Pour onto the cooked onion and pepper. Add the sun-dried tomatoes. Using the same bowl that you used to beat the eggs in, quickly mix the goats' cheese and crème fraiche together and randomly spoon this onto the egg mixture.
- Bake in the oven for 25–35 minutes, until the frittata is cooked.

Vegetable Chilli

Sauté pan or casserole dish

Olive oil

1 red onion, finely chopped

2–3 cloves of garlic, finely chopped

1 fresh chilli, finely chopped (choose according to desired strength!)

1 pepper, diced

2 carrots, diced

1 sweet potato, diced

2 courgettes, diced

80g mushrooms, quartered

1–2 teaspoons mild chilli powder

1–2 teaspoons paprika

1 tin of chopped tomatoes

1 tin of red kidney beans

1–2 teaspoons tomato purée

400ml vegetable stock or water (you can use half red wine, half water if you prefer)

- Heat the oil in a large sauté pan or casserole dish and fry the onion, garlic, chilli and pepper until they start to soften.
- Add the carrots and sweet potato and allow to sweat gently for 5–8 minutes. Add a drop of water if needed.
- Add the courgettes and mushrooms and cook for 2–3 minutes before adding the remaining ingredients.
- Cook gently on low/medium heat for 20 minutes, making sure the vegetables are tender.
- Serve with rice, corn chips or wraps.

Vegetable Stew with Herb Dumplings

You need to prepare the herb dumplings about 45 minutes before you are ready to serve the stew, to give them time to cook. If you like, you can make them in advance and keep them in the fridge until you need them.

Casserole dish or slow cooker

For the vegetable stew
Olive oil
I red onion, finely chopped
2 cloves of garlic, crushed
I leek, finely sliced
2 sticks of celery, finely sliced
2–3 carrots, sliced
I sweet potato, diced
I parsnip, sliced
I tin of chopped tomatoes

2 teaspoons tomato purée
500ml vegetable stock
2 teaspoons paprika
I bay leaf

For the herb dumplings
100g self-raising flour
50g suet
2–3 teaspoons mixed herbs
4 tablespoons water

To cook on the hob
- Heat the olive oil in a casserole dish and fry the onion, garlic and leek until the onion starts to soften.
- Add all the remaining stew ingredients. Turn the heat down to low and cook slowly for 1–1½ hours, adding the dumplings as below.

To cook in a slow cooker
- Preheat your slow cooker if necessary according to the manufacturer's instructions.
- Add all the stew ingredients (except the olive oil which isn't needed). Make sure the stock is warm when you add it as this will maintain the temperature. Turn your cooker to low and cook for 6–8 hours, adding the dumplings as below.

To make the herb dumplings
- Thoroughly mix the flour, suet and herbs together. Add the water gradually, a little at a time, to form a firm dough.
- Shape the dough into small balls and place these on top of the stew. Cover and leave for about 30 minutes, until the dumplings fluff up.
- Serve when the dumplings are ready.

Lentil and Vegetable Casserole

This is a really easy recipe and makes good use of any leftover vegetables you have in the fridge. You can also turn it into a lovely soup.

Slow cooker

1 onion, chopped

2–3 cloves of garlic, crushed

1 red pepper, diced

2 carrots, sliced

2 sticks of celery, sliced

1–2 leeks, finely sliced

2 sweet potatoes, diced

2–3 potatoes, diced

4 ripe tomatoes, finely chopped (you can use a small tin of chopped tomatoes if you prefer)

2–3 teaspoons sun-dried tomato paste

75g red lentils

75g brown lentils

1 teaspoon paprika

1 litre of vegetable stock

1 bay leaf

Seasoning to taste

- Preheat your slow cooker if necessary according to the manufacturer's instructions.
- Prepare all the vegetables.
- Place all the ingredients in the slow cooker. Make sure they are combined well and evenly distributed.
- Cover the vegetables with stock (you may need more than the 1 litre recommended, depending on the amount of vegetables used). Make sure the stock is warm when you add it as this will maintain the temperature.
- Set the slow cooker to low and cook for 6–8 hours, until the vegetables are tender.
- Season before serving.

Home-made Baked Beans

Casserole dish or sauté pan

150g dried haricot beans (or 2 tins of haricot beans)

Olive oil

1 onion, peeled and chopped

2 cloves of garlic

75ml apple juice

500g chopped tomatoes

Tomato purée to taste

A generous dash of Worcestershire sauce

1 teaspoon mustard

½ teaspoon cumin

A pinch of chilli powder

Seasoning to taste

- If using dried beans, soak them overnight in water. Next day, rinse the beans under cold running water and drain them. Bring to the boil in plenty of water. Boil fast for 10 minutes and then cover and simmer for 40 minutes or until soft. Drain away the water and keep the beans to one side. If using tinned beans, go straight to step 2.
- Heat the olive oil in a casserole dish or sauté pan and fry the onion and garlic until soft. Add the remaining ingredients, including the beans, and simmer on a low heat for 1 hour, stirring occasionally. Season to taste.

Red Kidney Bean Curry

Sauté pan or casserole dish

Olive oil

1 onion, chopped

2–3 cloves of garlic, crushed

1 chilli, finely chopped

2.5cm (1in) knuckle of ginger, finely chopped

1 teaspoon garam masala

1 teaspoon cumin seeds

1 teaspoon turmeric

1 stick of celery, finely sliced

1 red pepper, chopped

1 tin of red kidney beans

1 tin of chopped tomatoes

150ml stock or water

A small handful of coriander leaves

- Heat the oil in a deep pan and fry the onion, garlic, chilli and ginger for 3–4 minutes to help soften. Add the spices and cook for a further minute. (Be careful as this can cause quite a sharp aroma!)
- Add the celery and pepper and cook for another 2–3 minutes to help soften.
- Add the kidney beans, tinned tomatoes and water, with half the coriander leaves. Allow to cook on low/medium heat for 15–20 minutes.
- Just prior to serving, add the remaining coriander leaves.

Mixed Bean Casserole

Casserole dish or slow cooker

Olive oil

1 onion

2–3 cloves of garlic, crushed

1 red pepper, diced

1 fresh chilli, finely chopped

1 teaspoon cumin

1 teaspoon ground coriander

1 sweet potato, diced

1 tin of chopped tomatoes

1 tin of mixed beans

1 glass of red wine

300–500ml water or stock

1 bay leaf

Seasoning to taste

To cook on the hob

• Heat the oil and fry the onion and garlic for 1–2 minutes to help soften. Add the red pepper, chilli and spices. Cook for 1 minute more before adding the sweet potato. Sweat for 2–3 minutes.

• Add all the remaining ingredients, season to taste and cover the pan with a lid. Cook on a low heat for 1 hour.

• Remove the bay leaf before serving.

To cook in a slow cooker

• Preheat your slow cooker if necessary according to the manufacturer's instructions.

• Prepare the vegetables and place all the ingredients (except the olive oil which isn't needed) in the slow cooker. Make sure the stock is warm when you add it as this will maintain the temperature. Season to taste.

• Turn the slow cooker to high and cook for 6–7 hours, or until the vegetables are tender.

• Remove the bay leaf before serving.

Mushroom Risotto

Saucepan or casserole dish

10g dried porcini mushrooms

Olive oil

A knob of butter

1 onion, finely chopped

400g mixed mushrooms (shiitake, oyster, chestnut, wild etc.)

300g risotto rice

200ml white wine

500–700ml stock/mushroom water

A handful of fresh tarragon, chopped

Zest of ½ lemon

2–3 spoonfuls of low fat crème fraiche

A handful of fresh herbs, chopped

Grated Parmesan cheese to garnish

- Soak the porcini mushrooms as directed on the pack. This normally takes 20 minutes. Retain the fluid to add to your stock.
- Heat a splash of olive oil and a knob of butter in a saucepan and fry the onion until translucent. Add the fresh and dried mushrooms. Stir well.
- Stir in the rice, ensuring that it is completely covered in the oil/butter mixture. Don't let this stick! If necessary turn the heat down to medium.
- Add the wine and stir thoroughly. The wine will evaporate but will flavour the rice.
- Add the stock (ideally warm or hot stock) a little at a time. Wait until each addition of stock has been absorbed before adding more.
- After 10–15 minutes the rice should be tender (not soft as it should still have a little bite to it). After you have added all the stock, add the tarragon and lemon zest. Once all the stock is absorbed (the rice will reach a point where it cannot absorb any more liquid), stir in the crème fraiche.
- Serve immediately, garnished with freshly chopped herbs and grated Parmesan.

Squash, Sun-dried Tomato and Goats' Cheese Risotto

Saucepan or casserole dish

Olive oil

A knob of butter

1 onion, finely chopped

½ squash, cubed

300g risotto rice

200ml white wine

500–700ml vegetable stock

50g frozen peas, defrosted

50g sun-dried tomatoes, chopped

A handful of fresh, chopped herbs

120g goats' cheese, crumbled

Grated Parmesan cheese to garnish

- Heat a splash of olive oil and the butter in a saucepan and fry the onion until translucent. Add the cubed squash and stir well.
- Stir in the rice, ensuring that it is completely covered in the oil/butter mixture. Don't let this stick! If necessary turn the heat down to medium.
- Add the wine and stir thoroughly. The wine will evaporate but will flavour the rice.
- Add the stock (ideally warm or hot stock) a little at a time. Wait until each addition of stock has been absorbed before adding more.
- After 10 minutes add the peas and sun-dried tomatoes. After another 5 minutes the rice should be tender (not soft as it should still have a little bite to it). After you have added all the stock, add the freshly chopped herbs.
- Crumble on the goats' cheese. Serve immediately, garnished with chopped herbs and grated Parmesan.

Beetroot Risotto

This is a vibrant red risotto that looks really dramatic. Top with dark green lettuce leaves such as rocket to help emphasise the fabulous colour.

Saucepan or casserole dish

Olive oil

A knob of butter

1 onion, finely chopped

2 cloves of garlic, crushed

200g cooked beetroot, cut into chunks

300g risotto rice

200ml red wine

700ml stock

20g Parmesan cheese, grated

- Heat a splash of olive oil and the butter in a saucepan and fry the onion and garlic until translucent. Add the beetroot and stir well.
- Stir in the rice, ensuring that it is completely covered in the oil/butter mixture. Don't let this stick! If necessary turn the heat down to medium.
- Add the wine and stir thoroughly. The wine will evaporate but will flavour the rice.
- Add the stock (ideally warm or hot stock) a little at a time. Wait until each addition of stock has been absorbed before adding more.
- After 10–15 minutes the rice should be tender (not soft as it should still have a little bite to it). Add the grated Parmesan.
- Serve immediately.

Cheese, Mushroom and Courgette Layer Bake

Ovenproof dish

1 onion	100g Gruyère cheese (or you could use
2–3 cloves of garlic	mature Cheddar), grated
1 pack of tofu	3 courgettes
1 teaspoon dried parsley (or a small handful of	200g mushrooms
fresh)	75g breadcrumbs
1 teaspoon thyme	30g mature Cheddar, grated
2–3 tablespoons crème fraiche	Black pepper to taste

- Preheat the oven to 180°C/gas mark 4.
- Place the onion, garlic, tofu, herbs, crème fraiche and grated Gruyère cheese in a blender and mix until smooth. Season to taste.
- Chop the courgettes in half lengthways and the mushrooms into thick slices. Place the courgettes in the bottom of an ovenproof dish. Add a layer of the tofu and cheese cream, followed by a layer of mushrooms. Continue layering the cream and mushrooms, finishing with a cream layer.
- Sprinkle with breadcrumbs, grated Cheddar cheese and black pepper before baking in the oven for 30–35 minutes, until golden.

Potato and Cheese Bake

Ovenproof dish

1kg potatoes, cubed	50g Parmesan, grated
1 onion, finely chopped	A handful of chives, finely chopped
1–2 cloves of garlic, crushed	300ml low fat crème fraiche
100g mature Cheddar, grated	300ml double cream

- Preheat the oven to 180°C/gas mark 4.
- Steam the potatoes until almost tender.
- Grease the ovenproof dish with butter. Layer the potatoes, onion and garlic with the cheese and chives.
- Mix the crème fraiche and cream together (you can use 100% double cream if you prefer), and pour over the potato and cheese mix.
- Finish with a sprinkle of cheese before baking in the oven for 15–20 minutes.

Creamy Mushroom Tagliatelle

Sauté pan and saucepan

350g tagliatelle	150g chestnut or wild mushrooms
A dash of olive oil	½ jar of pesto
20g butter	1 tub of cream cheese
1 small onion, very finely chopped	100ml milk
2 cloves of garlic, very finely chopped	Parmesan cheese, grated

- Cook the tagliatelle according to the instructions on the packet. While it is cooking, heat the olive oil and butter and fry the finely chopped onion and garlic until the onion starts to soften.
- Add the mushrooms and cook for another few minutes until they are soft but not soggy.
- Add the pesto, cream cheese and milk and keep stirring until this forms a creamy sauce.
- Drain the pasta and add to the creamy sauce. Stir well until evenly distributed.
- Garnish with Parmesan cheese.

Quorn and Mushroom Stroganoff

Sauté pan

Olive oil

1 onion, finely chopped

2–3 cloves of garlic, crushed

300g Quorn chunks

300g mushrooms, sliced

2–3 teaspoons paprika

2–3 teaspoons Dijon mustard

100ml white wine

2 teaspoons fresh parsley

100ml stock

150ml crème fraiche

- Heat the oil in a large sauté pan and fry the onion and garlic for 1 minute. Add the Quorn and cook for 3–4 minutes.
- Add the mushrooms, paprika and mustard; stir well, before adding the wine. Some of this will evaporate as you continue to cook for a couple of minutes.
- Add the parsley and stock and cook on a low heat for 15 minutes.
- Just before serving, remove from the heat and stir in the crème fraiche to form a creamy sauce. Serve on a bed of white rice.

Chinese Stir-fried Vegetables

Wok or sauté pan

2 cloves of garlic, crushed

Zest of 1 lemon

2.5cm (1in) knuckle of ginger, grated

15ml vinegar

2 tablespoons honey

75ml soy sauce

Olive oil

1 red pepper, sliced

1 green pepper, sliced

1–2 carrots, cut into sticks

1 bunch of spring onions, thickly sliced

1 courgette, cut into sticks

3 sticks of celery, sliced

150g mushrooms, sliced

100g almonds

- Blend the garlic, lemon zest, ginger, vinegar, honey and soy sauce together. Leave to one side.
- Heat the oil in the wok or sauté pan and add all the vegetables.
- Stir-fry on high heat for 2–3 minutes before adding the almonds and the soy sauce mixture.
- Cook for a further couple of minutes before serving.

Goats' Cheese, Brown Lentil and Rocket Salad

This is one of my absolute favourite salads. The flavours really complement each other and it is surprisingly filling.

Saucepan and serving bowl

175g Puy lentils

100g rocket

1 small punnet of cherry tomatoes

1 red onion, sliced

125g goats' cheese, crumbled

For the dressing

2 tablespoons olive oil

2 tablespoons balsamic vinegar

Seasoning to taste

- Place the lentils in boiling water and cook for 15 minutes until soft. Drain and leave to one side.
- Make the dressing by mixing together the olive oil and balsamic vinegar. Season to taste.
- Place the rocket, tomatoes, onion, lentils and goats' cheese in a larger serving bowl. Stir well before pouring over the dressing.
- Serve immediately.

Halloween Casserole

This has a wonderful colour and is a perfect winter warmer. You can use pumpkin or any other squash.

Casserole dish

Olive oil

1 onion, chopped

2–3 cloves of garlic, crushed

2–4cm (1–1½in) knuckle of ginger, finely chopped

½ chilli, finely chopped (optional)

1 teaspoon cumin seeds

1 red pepper, sliced

1 large potato, diced

1 sweet potato, diced

1 large carrot, sliced

25g butter

Flesh of 1 small squash or pumpkin, diced

2 sticks of celery, sliced

75g red lentils

1 tin of chopped tomatoes

1 bay leaf

1 teaspoon paprika

500ml vegetable stock

Seasoning to taste

- Heat the olive oil in a large casserole dish and soften the onion, garlic, ginger, chilli, cumin seeds and red pepper for 2–3 minutes.
- Add the potatoes, carrot, butter and squash. Allow to sweat for 5 minutes.
- Add all the remaining ingredients. Cover and cook on low/medium heat for 30–40 minutes until the vegetables are soft.
- Remove the bay leaf and season to taste before serving.

Spicy Rice

I love rice dishes, particularly those made with pilau or spicy rice. This can be used as a side dish or a main meal.

Sauté pan

Olive oil

1 onion, chopped

2 cloves of garlic, crushed

2.5–5cm (1–2in) of fresh ginger, grated

1 pepper, chopped

1 red chilli, chopped (optional)

1 teaspoon coriander

1 teaspoon cardamom

1 teaspoon ground cumin

1 teaspoon turmeric

½ teaspoon ground nutmeg

1 bay leaf

1 cinnamon stick

250g basmati rice

75g red lentils

750ml (1¼ pints) water

75g peas (thawed if frozen)

50g sweetcorn

25g sliced almonds

A small handful of fresh coriander leaves (optional)

- Heat the olive oil in a large sauté or casserole pan and fry the onion, garlic, ginger, pepper and chilli for 2 minutes to soften.
- Add the herbs and spices (apart from the bay leaf and cinnamon stick) and cook for a further 2–3 minutes.
- Add the rice and lentils and stir well ensuring the flavours start to mix with the rice. Top with the water.
- Add the cinnamon stick and bay leaf and cover. Cook for 10 minutes on medium heat.
- Turn off the heat. Add the peas, sweetcorn, almond slices and coriander leaves. Stir and cover again and leave for 10 minutes.
- Loosen with a fork before serving.

Lentil Loaf

Loaf tin

150g lentils

1 onion, finely chopped

2 cloves of garlic

50g oats

75g cooked rice

1 pepper, red or green, diced

1 teaspoon mixed herbs

A pinch of cayenne pepper

2 tomatoes, chopped

Tomato purée to taste (optional)

Seasoning to taste

- Preheat the oven to 180°C/gas mark 4.
- Boil the lentils until soft. Drain, reserving the water.
- Stir in the remaining ingredients to form a thick mixture, not too wet. Use the retained stock if the mixture is too dry.
- Pour into a greased 450g (1lb) loaf tin and cover with foil.
- Bake in the oven for 30 minutes.
- Serve with roast potatoes and vegetables as an alternative to meat.

Quorn and Mushroom Crumble

Sauté pan and ovenproof dish

Olive oil

1 onion, finely chopped

2 cloves of garlic, crushed

200g Quorn chunks

150g chestnut mushrooms

1 tub of cream cheese

250ml milk

½ teaspoon tarragon

½ teaspoon parsley

Seasoning to taste

30g sunflower seeds

30g pumpkin seeds

50g oats

50g plain flour

1 teaspoon mixed herbs

50g Parmesan cheese, grated

25g butter

- Preheat the oven to 180°C/gas mark 4.
- Heat the olive oil in a sauté pan and fry the onion and garlic until the onion starts to soften. Add the Quorn and mushrooms and cook for another 5 minutes.
- Add the cream cheese and milk and allow the cream cheese to melt, forming a creamy sauce. Add the tarragon and parsley and season. If you want more sauce, add a spoonful or two of crème fraiche. Remove from the heat.
- Put the seeds, oats, flour, herbs and grated Parmesan cheese in a bowl. Rub in the butter to form more of a breadcrumb mix. Season.
- Pour the mushroom and Quorn mixture into the ovenproof dish. Top with the crumble mix and bake in the oven for 20 minutes until golden.

Thai Rice

Saucepan or sauté pan

Olive oil

1 onion, chopped

2 cloves of garlic, crushed

2.5cm (1in) piece of ginger, finely sliced

1 chilli, finely sliced (optional)

2.5cm (1in) knuckle of galangal, finely sliced
(optional)

1 small stick of lemon grass

1 teaspoon coriander seeds

1 teaspoon cumin seeds

Zest and juice of 2 limes

225g basmati rice

750ml water or vegetable stock

A handful of fresh coriander

- Heat the olive oil in a heavy-based pan and fry the onion, garlic, ginger, chilli, galangal and lemon grass for 2 minutes. Add the coriander and cumin seeds and cook for another minute.
- Add the zest from the limes (retaining the juice for later). Add the rice and stir for 1–2 minutes before gradually adding the water or stock.
- Cook on medium/high heat for 5 minutes. Turn down to low for a further 5 minutes, then cover the pan with a lid and remove from the heat for 10 minutes.
- Check the rice is cooked; fluff it up with a fork before adding the chopped coriander and lime juice.

Pease Pudding

My husband loves pease pudding. I sometimes make it in the slow cooker, but this recipe is for the saucepan. Traditional recipes tell you to cook the pease pudding in muslin cloth, but I really can't be bothered with that, so here is my variation. You may have to adjust the amount of water as this can absorb fluids very quickly.

Saucepan

300g yellow or green split peas	Sprigs of parsley and thyme
1 onion, peeled and cut in half	1–1½ litres of water
2–3 cloves of garlic, crushed	25g butter
125g celeriac, peeled and roughly chopped	Black pepper to taste

- Soak the split peas in water overnight. Rinse well before using to remove any scum.
- Place the split peas in a large pan with the onion, garlic, celeriac, herbs and water. Bring to the boil, cover and simmer for 45 minutes to 1 hour – add more water if needed as this can go dry. Remove the vegetables and herbs.
- You now need to reduce the split peas until they are tender enough to form a mush. Do this by cooking them gently, monitoring the liquid level until the water is absorbed and the split peas form a mush. Add a little water if the mixture is too dry. Add the butter and season well.
- Serve immediately or reheat in the saucepan when you are ready. If the pease pudding has dried out, add a little butter to help soften it.

Lentil Dahl

This is so easy to make and costs very little. You can make it mild and creamy by adding some Greek yoghurt – ideal for children – or spice it up to suit your taste.

Saucepan or casserole dish

Olive oil

1 onion, chopped

2 cloves garlic, crushed

2.5–5cm (1–2in) knuckle of fresh ginger, chopped

1 pepper, chopped (optional)

2–3 teaspoons mild or sweet curry powder or paste

1–2 teaspoons turmeric

1 teaspoon ground ginger

1–2 tomatoes, finely chopped

1 teaspoon tomato purée

100g red lentils

300–400ml water

Coconut to garnish

- Heat the oil in a large pan and fry the onion, garlic, fresh ginger and pepper until soft.
- Add the curry powder/paste, turmeric, ground ginger, tomatoes and tomato purée and cook for another 2 minutes.
- Add the lentils and cover with the water. Simmer gently. Add more water if necessary.
- Sprinkle with coconut before serving.

Mushroom and Cashew Nut Roast

This is so much easier if you have a food processor that chops food. If so, you can make it in minutes; otherwise you will drive yourself nuts (excuse the pun!) with all that chopping. I have many friends who are meat eaters and they all love this recipe. You can freeze this (before baking) and use it when needed.

Sauté pan and loaf tin

Olive oil	200g cashew nuts, chopped
1 onion, finely chopped	2 teaspoons yeast extract
250g mushrooms (I like chestnut but choose whatever you prefer)	50g home-made breadcrumbs

- Preheat the oven to 180°C/gas mark 4.
- Heat a little oil in a pan and fry the onion until translucent.
- Add the mushrooms and nuts and cook for 5 minutes.
- Add the yeast extract, followed by the breadcrumbs, and stir well.
- Spoon the mixture into a lined 450g (1lb) loaf tin and press down to form a firm base.
- At this stage you can freeze the dish if you like and use when needed.
- If you are using the dish immediately, bake in the oven for 40 minutes.

Variation

Wrap the mixture in half a pack of ready-made puff pastry to make a Mushroom en Croûte. This looks very impressive, particularly for Christmas lunch or as an alternative to meat when cooking a roast dinner. Roll out the pastry into a rectangle 30cm (12in) wide by 40cm (16in) long and place on a greased baking tray. Spoon the mixture into the middle of the pastry lengthways. Using a sharp knife, cut 2.5–5cm (1–2in) strips either side of the mixture – you will then fold these over the mixture to form a pleated effect. Fold the pastry over the top of the filling and seal well with beaten egg or milk. Bake for 40 minutes until the pastry is golden.

Tip

Make double the amount of mixture to make one nut roast and a Mushroom en Croûte. Freeze both, uncooked, until needed.

Spinach and Ricotta Lasagne

Quick and easy, this recipe will nevertheless impress your family and friends. If you are in a hurry and don't want to prepare your own pasta sauce, Seeds of Change Cherry Tomato and Parmesan makes a good alternative, with a lovely home-made flavour.

Mixing bowl and ovenproof dish

1 onion, finely chopped	Black pepper to season
1 pot of ricotta	Lasagne sheets
100g mature Cheddar, grated	1 jar of pasta sauce
150g fresh spinach leaves (baby spinach is best)	Grated Parmesan or other cheese for topping
Grated nutmeg	

- Preheat the oven to 200°C/gas mark 6.
- Place the onion, ricotta and grated cheese in a bowl and mix well. Add the spinach leaves (if you place the spinach in a colander and rinse it under a hot tap for a few seconds it softens the leaves and makes the mixing easier).
- Once mixed, add some grated nutmeg and season with black pepper.
- Place a small layer of ricotta mixture in the bottom of a lasagne dish, followed by a layer of lasagne sheets. Top with a small layer of pasta sauce. Continue with a layer of ricotta, then lasagne, and finally the remaining pasta sauce. Add approximately 50ml of water to the empty sauce jar, rinse the jar and pour the water over the top of the lasagne.
- Grate some Parmesan or other cheese onto the lasagne before baking in the oven for 30–40 minutes.
- Serve with potato wedges and salad – delicious!

Spicy Red Cabbage

This is perfect to liven up your Christmas lunch. But don't just make it at Christmas; use it to add colour and flavour to your meals throughout the year. It is cheap and easy to prepare.

Slow cooker or casserole dish

1 red cabbage, shredded	1 teaspoon dried cardamom
2 onions, chopped	25g soft brown sugar
2 Bramley apples, peeled (if you prefer), cored and chopped	Rind and juice of 1 orange
4 teaspoons cinnamon powder	50ml apple juice
1 teaspoon mixed spice	1 glass/200ml of red wine

To cook on the hob
- Prepare the cabbage, onions and apples (I leave the peel on the apples, but it is up to you).
- Place in the casserole dish with all the remaining ingredients and mix thoroughly.
- Cook on a low heat for approximately 1 hour until the cabbage is soft. Stir occasionally.
- Serve as a side vegetable dish. If you make a large batch don't waste it; you can bottle it to preserve until needed.

To cook in a slow cooker
- Preheat your slow cooker if necessary according to the manufacturer's instructions.
- Prepare the cabbage, onions and apples (I leave the peel on the apples, but it is up to you).
- Place in the slow cooker with all the remaining ingredients and mix thoroughly.
- Turn the slow cooker to low and cook for 6–8 hours (or high for 4 hours) until the cabbage is soft. Stir occasionally.
- Serve as a side vegetable dish. If you make a large batch don't waste it; you can bottle it to preserve until needed.

Chickpea and Vegetable Casserole

Casserole dish or slow cooker

Olive oil

1 onion, sliced

1–2 cloves of garlic, crushed

1–2 chillies (optional)

1 pepper, sliced

2 sticks of celery, sliced

1 sweet potato, diced

1 white potato, diced

2 carrots, sliced

2 courgettes, sliced

400g tin chopped tomatoes

1 teaspoon paprika

1 teaspoon ground coriander

1 teaspoon fenugreek (optional)

400g tin chickpeas

500ml water or stock

1 bay leaf

Fresh herbs to taste

Seasoning to taste

To cook on the hob

- Heat the oil in a large ovenproof dish and fry the onion and garlic, stirring well, until they start to soften.
- Add the chillies, pepper, celery, potatoes, carrots and courgettes. Cook for another 5 minutes, stirring well to prevent sticking. If necessary, add a few drops of water.
- Add all the remaining ingredients. Cover with a lid and cook on a low heat for 45 minutes. Check halfway through to ensure there is enough fluid in the casserole. Add more water or stock as necessary.
- Add fresh herbs to taste and season well before serving.

To cook in a slow cooker

- Preheat your slow cooker according to the manufacturer's instructions.
- Meanwhile, prepare the vegetables. Add all the ingredients (except the olive oil which isn't needed) to the slow cooker. Make sure the stock is warm when you add it as this will maintain the temperature. Set the slow cooker to high and cook for 6 hours, until the vegetables are tender.
- Add the fresh herbs 15 minutes before serving. Season to taste.

Ratatouille

This is so easy — and versatile, too. You can serve it on its own with some warm crusty bread, or mixed with pasta to create a more filling dish.

Casserole dish

Olive oil

1 aubergine, diced

2 courgettes, sliced

1 red onion, sliced

1–2 cloves of garlic, crushed

1–2 red peppers, sliced

400g chopped tomatoes

2 teaspoons tomato purée

100ml red wine

A handful of chopped fresh herbs

- Heat the olive oil in a large ovenproof dish and fry the aubergine and courgettes for 5 minutes until slightly charred. Remove and place on a plate until later.
- Add the onion, garlic and peppers and cook for 3–4 minutes.
- Add the tomatoes, tomato purée and wine.
- Add the aubergines and courgettes. Cover the pan with a lid. Turn down the heat to low and cook slowly for 15 minutes until the mixture reduces slightly.
- Add fresh herbs prior to serving.

Curried Potato and Black-eyed Beans

Casserole dish

Olive oil

1 teaspoon cumin seeds

2 teaspoons ground cinnamon

1 teaspoon turmeric powder

1 chilli, finely chopped

1 red onion

1–2 cloves garlic, crushed

½ red pepper, chopped

750g potatoes, cubed

300ml water

2 bay leaves

400g tin of chopped tomatoes

300g cooked black-eyed beans (or tinned)

Juice of 1 lemon

1 tablespoon fresh coriander

- Heat a dash of olive oil in a deep-based pan or casserole dish. Add the spices and chilli, Stir-fry for 1 minute.
- Add the onion, garlic and red pepper and cook until soft.
- Add the potatoes and sweat for a further 5 minutes.
- Add all the remaining ingredients (except the fresh coriander), cover and cook on a low heat for approximately 1 hour, until tender.
- Garnish with fresh coriander before serving.

Green Bean and Tomato Bredie

A bredie is a Cape stew. Serve with fresh salad and rice.

Casserole dish

Olive oil

2 cloves of garlic, chopped

1 teaspoon fresh ginger, grated

½ teaspoon ground ginger

1 small chilli, finely chopped

2 onions, chopped

2 carrots, chopped into chunks

400g potatoes, chopped into chunks

400g chopped tinned tomatoes

200ml water

200g green beans cut into 2–3 pieces

3–4 chard leaves, torn into a few pieces

1 tablespoon fresh coriander

Seasoning to taste

- Heat the olive oil in a pan and fry the garlic, ginger, chilli and onions until the onions soften.
- Add the carrots and potatoes and sweat for a further 5 minutes, stirring constantly.
- Add the tomatoes and water, cover and cook on a low heat for 45 minutes.
- Add the green beans, chard and coriander and continue to cook until the vegetables are tender and the liquid has reduced.
- Season and serve.

Black-eyed Bean Chilli

Sauté pan or casserole dish

Olive oil

1 large onion, chopped

1–2 cloves of garlic, crushed

1–2 chillies

1 small red pepper, finely chopped

1 teaspoon chilli powder (or to taste)

¼ teaspoon cayenne pepper (optional)

1–2 teaspoons oregano

1 carrot, finely chopped

400g tin of chopped tomatoes

1 tin of black-eyed beans

200–300ml water

Seasoning to taste

- Heat the oil in a pan and fry the onion, garlic, chilli and pepper until soft.
- Add the spices and cook for 1 more minute.
- Add all the remaining ingredients. Cover with a lid and leave to cook on a low heat for 45 minutes.
- Check occasionally to see if the mixture needs more fluid. Season to taste.
- Serve with sour cream and rice or tortillas.

Vegetable Curry

Casserole dish or sauté pan

Olive oil

1 large onion, finely chopped

2.5cm (1in) piece of fresh ginger, thinly sliced

2–3 cloves of garlic, crushed

2 tablespoons of mild or medium curry
   powder (depending on taste)

1 chilli (optional)

1 red pepper, chopped

4 ripe tomatoes, finely chopped

1 sweet potato, cubed

1 large white potato, cubed

150g yellow split peas

500ml water

2 handfuls of baby leaf spinach

A handful of fresh coriander, roughly shredded

- Heat the oil in a large casserole or deep sauté pan and fry the onion, ginger and garlic. Cook for 1 minute before adding the curry powder and chilli. (This can give off quite a fierce aroma so don't stand too close to the pan!) If the mixture is too dry, add a touch of water.
- Add the pepper, tomatoes and potatoes. Stir together and allow to cook gently for 5 minutes.
- Add the split peas and water. Cover with a lid and cook gently for 20–30 minutes.
- Add the spinach and coriander and cook for a further 5 minutes before serving.

One Pot Essentials

This chapter contains basic recipe ideas, sauces, dips and pâtés to help you create some extra dishes and enhance some of your family favourites. Knowing how to make the perfect white sauce will open up many more recipe ideas for you – add some cheese and you have a base for cauliflower or macaroni cheese. Add some parsley to the white sauce and you have the perfect accompaniment to some slow cooked ham. Although these are not technically one pot recipes, they will, I hope, prove to be an invaluable guide for you.

Pastry

Basic Pastry Recipe

When you are making pastry, remember the rules: half fat to flour; always use cold water; try to handle the pastry as little as possible.

200g plain flour   Cold water
100g butter

To make by hand
• Place the flour in a large bowl and add small pieces of the chilled butter. Using your fingertips, rub the butter into the flour until the whole mix resembles breadcrumbs.
• Mix in 5–6 tablespoons of cold water (a little at a time) until the mixture forms a dough. Wrap the dough in cling film and leave in the fridge to cool until needed.

To make in a food processor
• Place the flour and butter in the processor and whizz for a few seconds.
• Add 5–6 tablespoons of water, gradually, while the machine is on, until the mixture forms a ball of dough. Wrap the dough in cling film and leave in the fridge to cool until needed.

Note: If you prefer a flakier pastry, freeze the butter and grate it into the flour. Continue as above.

Cinnamon and Orange Sweet Pastry Recipe

250g plain flour	2 teaspoons cinnamon powder
125g butter	Zest of 1 orange
75g caster sugar or icing sugar	Orange juice

- It is easier to make this pastry in a food processor. Add the flour, butter, caster or icing sugar, cinnamon and orange zest and whizz for a couple of seconds.
- Add the orange juice slowly until the dough forms. Leave the dough in the fridge to cool for 5 minutes before using as normal.

Sauces

Basic White Sauce

25g butter	500–750ml milk
1 tablespoon plain flour or cornflour	Black pepper to taste

- Melt the butter gently in a saucepan on medium heat (not high!). Add the flour or cornflour and stir well with a wooden spoon. Add the milk, a little at a time, continuing to stir to avoid lumps.
- Switch now to a balloon whisk. Continue to stir over a medium heat until the sauce begins to thicken. The balloon whisk will also help eradicate any lumps that may have materialised. Add more milk as necessary to get the desired thickness. The sauce should be the thickness of custard.
- Season with black pepper.

Cheese Sauce

This is also known as Mornay

25g butter
1 tablespoon of plain flour or cornflour
500–750ml milk
75g mature cheese, grated

2 tablespoons nutritional yeast flakes (optional)
½ teaspoon mustard
Black pepper to taste

- Melt the butter gently in a saucepan on medium heat (not high!). Add the flour or cornflour and stir well with a wooden spoon. Add the milk, a little at a time, continuing to stir to avoid lumps.
- Switch now to a balloon whisk. Continue to stir over a medium heat until the sauce begins to thicken. The balloon whisk will also help eradicate any lumps that may have materialised. Add more milk as necessary to get the desired thickness. The sauce should be the thickness of custard.
- Add the grated cheese and mustard and stir well. If you are using nutritional yeast flakes, add these first as you may then find you need less cheese – taste as you go!
- Season with black pepper.

Parsley Sauce

25g butter
1 tablespoon of plain flour or cornflour
500–750ml milk

A handful of fresh parsley, finely chopped
Black pepper to taste

- Melt the butter gently in a saucepan on medium heat (not high!). Add the flour or cornflour and stir well with a wooden spoon. Add the milk, a little at a time, continuing to stir to avoid lumps.
- Switch now to a balloon whisk. Continue to stir over a medium heat until the sauce begins to thicken. The balloon whisk will also help eradicate any lumps that may have materialised. Add more milk as necessary to get the desired thickness. The sauce should be the thickness of custard.
- Add the parsley and season with black pepper.

Bread Sauce

This is best made with old or slightly stale bread. You can crumble the bread with your fingers to produce small pieces or, if you prefer a smoother sauce, whizz into breadcrumbs (any unused breadcrumbs can be frozen until needed for other dishes).

1 onion, finely chopped	500ml milk
4 whole cloves	Seasoning to taste
5–8 peppercorns	50–75g breadcrumbs (see above)
1–2 bay leaves	100ml single cream (optional)

- Place the onion, cloves, peppercorns, bay leaves and milk in a pan.
- Slowly bring the milk to the boil and simmer gently for 5 minutes. Remove from the heat and leave to one side to infuse (you can leave this while your roast cooks).
- Five minutes before you are ready to serve, reheat the milk gently. Remove the cloves, peppercorns and bay leaves. Season to taste before adding your crumbled bread – a little at a time until you get the desired consistency.
- Remove from the heat, stir in the cream if you prefer a creamier consistency, sprinkle with nutmeg and serve.

Tomato and Herb Sauce

If I am making something with a tomato sauce base, I double up the recipe and then store half in the fridge. This can then be used as a pizza topping, pasta sauce or addition to any other savoury dish. Here is a basic recipe for you to add to.

Olive oil

2–3 cloves of garlic, finely chopped

2 red onions, finely chopped

1 kg tomatoes (I prefer fresh, ripe tomatoes, but you can use 2–3 tins of tomatoes)

½ red pepper, chopped

1–2 splashes of balsamic vinegar

1–2 splashes of red wine

A handful of fresh herbs

Seasoning to taste

- Heat the olive oil in a pan and fry the garlic and onions until translucent.
- Chop the tomatoes. I never peel my tomatoes as I think it an unnecessary faff. However, if you prefer to peel them, take a sharp knife and lightly scour the edges of the tomatoes. Place them in a bowl of boiling water until the skins start to curl slightly. Remove from the water and peel off the skins before chopping.
- Add the tomatoes and red pepper to the onions. Cook for 1–2 minutes before adding the balsamic and red wine. Simmer gently for 10 minutes.
- Add the fresh herbs (these can be basil, thyme or oregano), or you can use fresh frozen herb cubes.
- Season to taste.

Slow-baked Tomatoes

Strictly speaking this is not a sauce, dip or salsa, but I have placed it with the sauces as I use it so often in a variety of meals. You can use this as a quick and easy pasta sauce, a topping for a pizza, an accompaniment to a meat, fish or vegetable dish or in a salad. The sweetness of the tomatoes alongside the hit of basil and garlic is truly heaven. I bake this in large batches, especially when I have ripe tomatoes that need using up, or if I see cherry tomatoes on special offer. You can then store them in jars (covered in olive oil) or in an airtight container in the fridge for one week maximum.

A batch of ripe tomatoes, halved

4 cloves of garlic, crushed (more if preferred)

A sprinkle of balsamic vinegar

A drizzle of olive oil

A handful of fresh herbs

I teaspoon sugar

I teaspoon salt

- Preheat the oven to 50–100°C/gas mark ¼ (very low).
- Place the tomatoes in a baking tray. Sprinkle on the garlic, sugar, salt and balsamic vinegar. Finish with a drizzle of olive oil.
- Bake in the oven for 2–3 hours or slow cooker for 4 hours on low.
- When the tomatoes are cooked, add a handful of fresh herbs. I prefer oregano or basil.
- Use or store as required.

Pesto

I love pesto, and at almost £2 for a small jar, it is great to make your own, especially if you have some fresh herbs that need using up. This recipe uses the traditional basil leaves, but you can try coriander for a variation in flavour.

2–3 handfuls of basil	25g Parmesan cheese, grated
1–2 cloves of garlic, crushed	Olive oil
25g pine nuts	Seasoning to taste

- I use a small food processor and mix all the ingredients together thoroughly. Add olive oil until you are happy with the consistency.
- Leave to rest for 20–30 minutes to help enhance the flavours.
- Serve with pasta, mashed potato, salads, dips or even as a topping or marinade.

Fruit Sauce

I made this sauce one Christmas as a bit of an experiment to go with some pink pears. My mum loved it and it has now become a family favourite.

2 teaspoons cornflour	Grated nutmeg
250ml orange juice	½ teaspoon vanilla essence
Zest of 1 orange	
1 teaspoon cinnamon	

- Mix the cornflour with 50ml of the juice. Stir well.
- Gently heat the rest of the juice and add all the remaining ingredients. Gradually add the cornflour mix. Stir continuously.
- Cook on a low heat until the sauce is thick and smooth.
- Serve with fresh fruit, pies or crumble.

Gravy

I know most people tend to grab the gravy granules but home-made gravy really is simple. If you are making bangers and mash, nothing beats the flavour of home-made onion gravy. Here are some recipes to help motivate you.

Onion Gravy

A dash of oil (you can use the fat from a roast)
A small knob of butter
4 red onions, finely chopped
I clove garlic, crushed
5 tablespoons red wine vinegar (or balsamic will do)

I tablespoon flour
I teaspoon Marmite or yeast extract (optional)
350ml stock (I use homemade vegetable stock, but you can use whatever you prefer)

- Combine the oil and butter as this prevents the butter from burning. Fry the onions and garlic in a pan on a low heat until very soft – this usually takes about 15–20 minutes, so remember to allow this time when cooking your roast or bangers and mash.
- Add the red wine vinegar and cook until the liquid is reduced by half.
- Stir in the flour and Marmite. Add the stock, a little at a time, and stir well. Cook gently, allowing the gravy to thicken. You can add more water or stock if it is too thick.

Red Wine Gravy

I tablespoon plain flour or cornflour
300ml hot meat stock (if roasting a joint, use the meat juices for this)

2 teaspoons redcurrant jelly
300ml red wine
Seasoning to taste

- Place the flour in a saucepan, add a little stock and stir well over a gentle heat. Add the redcurrant jelly and continue to add more stock as the gravy thickens.
- Add the wine and season to taste. Continue to cook until the gravy thickens to the desired consistency (about 8–10 minutes).

Stocks

I will probably make good chefs cry but I don't often use stocks; I find water and a good selection of herbs and spices does the trick. However, there are certain dishes where it really does add good flavour. I don't buy stock cubes as I find they tend to give food an overpowering salty taste. It's better to make your own using any leftover vegetables – even if they are well past their best. Bottle the stock and store it in the fridge, or freeze it in a suitable container until required.

Vegetable Stocks

There really is no recipe for stock – anything goes. I normally raid my vegetable drawer and pull out any food that is no longer suitable for fresh vegetable dishes. I also include some of the vegetables we would normally throw away, which I have saved up over a few days, as it still has lots of flavour. Don't use anything from the brassica family as it will make your stock smell – so no cauliflower, cabbage, broccoli etc.

- Place your chosen ingredients in a stock pan and cover with water. Add any chosen herbs and seasoning.
- Allow to simmer, and then reduce the heat to low and leave to cook on a very low heat for 1–2 hours.
- Strain and retain the liquid. Bottle and store in the fridge for up to four days or freeze in a suitable container for up to three months.

Note: Use the same principle to make **Fish Stock** or **Meat Stock**. You can use the whole carcass of the animal or bird, including the bones, and even the heads of fish, so there is no waste. If you are making a meat stock, stick to one animal or bird source. Add wine and vegetables that suit the stock you are making. Remember to strain the stock thoroughly before bottling and make sure you label and date it, especially if you are freezing it.

Pie and Mash Shop Liquor

My husband was raised in south-east London so is a big fan of the traditional Manzies Pie and Mash Shops. The pie liquor looks a bit dubious but tastes divine. Here is a variation to the traditional recipe.

25g butter

25g flour or cornflour

200ml water

100ml white wine

A large bunch of fresh parsley, finely chopped

Seasoning to taste

- Melt the butter in a pan over a medium heat. Add the flour or cornflour and stir continuously with a wooden spoon.
- Gradually add the water, stirring well. When approximately half the water is added, switch to a hand whisk. Keep stirring to remove any lumps.
- Add the remaining water and the wine and continue to stir.
- Add the chopped parsley and season to taste.
- Continue to heat the liquor until it starts to thicken. You don't want this too thick; it should be the consistency of gravy.

Butters

Butters can be used on fish, but also to add flavour to a jacket potato, bread or even soup. They can be made in advance and stored in an airtight container in the fridge (or an old margarine container), or they can be frozen until needed. I have frozen them in silicone ice-cube trays as they are simple to remove and in handy-sized portions. Remember to label the butters clearly.

150g butter

1 tablespoon of fresh herbs or 1–2 teaspoons of dried

- Mix the butter and herbs together thoroughly.
- Store in an airtight container until needed. If you want to use this immediately, wait at least 30 minutes to allow the butter to absorb the herb flavours.

Garlic Butter

150g butter	1 tablespoon of fresh herbs or 1–2 teaspoons
2–3 garlic cloves, crushed	of dried

- Mix the butter, garlic and herbs together thoroughly.
- Store in an airtight container until needed. If you want to use this immediately, wait at least 30 minutes to allow the butter to absorb the flavours.

Ginger and Lime Butter

150g butter	Zest and juice of 1 lime
2.5cm (1in) knuckle of ginger, grated	A dash of cayenne pepper (optional)

- Mix the butter, ginger, lime and cayenne pepper together thoroughly.
- Store in an airtight container until needed. If you want to use this immediately, wait at least 30 minutes to allow the butter to absorb the flavours.

Chilli Butter

150g butter	A dash of Tabasco sauce
1–2 chillies, finely chopped	

- Mix the butter, chillies and Tabasco together thoroughly.
- Store in an airtight container until needed. If you want to use this immediately, wait at least 30 minutes to allow the butter to absorb the flavours.

Dips

Dips have become increasingly popular but can be expensive to buy ready made. Why not make your own? They are quick and easy and you'll save money.

Mackerel Pâté

This is a very easy recipe that can be prepared in seconds.

---

4 mackerel fillets, boned and ready to eat
I small tub of low fat cream cheese
Juice and zest of I lemon

A handful of fresh parsley, chopped
Seasoning to taste

- Make sure your mackerel fillets are free from bones and skin. If you are not sure about this, ask your fishmonger to do it for you.
- Place all the ingredients in a liquidiser or small food processor. Whizz for a few seconds until the ingredients have blended well.
- Season to taste.
- Allow to settle for at least 20 minutes for the flavours to infuse before serving.

Hummus

400g chickpeas (you can use canned)
2–3 tablespoons olive oil or flax oil (great to get some omega into your diet)
Juice of ½ a lemon

2–4 cloves of garlic, depending on personal taste
I tablespoon tahini paste (made from sesame seeds)

- Place all the ingredients into a blender and whizz until smooth. Add more lemon juice or olive oil until you get the desired consistency.
- If you taste this and think it is not garlicky enough, don't be tempted to add more until you have let it rest for at least 20 minutes. Then taste again and add more if you think it needs it.
- Store in an airtight container in the fridge. The hummus should last 3–4 days.

Pesto Hummus

400g chickpeas (you can use canned)
2–3 tablespoons olive oil or flax oil (great to get some omega into your diet)
Juice of ½ lemon
2–4 cloves of garlic, depending on personal taste
1 tablespoon tahini paste (made from sesame seeds)
1 tablespoon pesto

- Place all the ingredients into a blender and whizz until smooth. Add more lemon juice or olive oil until you get the desired consistency.
- If you taste this and think it is not garlicky enough, don't be tempted to add more until you have let it rest for at least 20 minutes. Then taste again and add more if you think it needs it.
- Store in an airtight container in the fridge. The hummus should last 3–4 days.

Red Pepper Hummus

400g chickpeas (you can use canned)
2–3 tablespoons olive oil or flax oil (great to get some omega into your diet)
Juice of ½ lemon
1 sweet red pepper
2–4 cloves of garlic, depending on personal taste
1 tablespoon tahini paste (made from sesame seeds)

- Place all the ingredients into a blender and whizz until smooth. Add more lemon juice or olive oil until you get the desired consistency.
- If you taste this and think it is not garlicky enough, don't be tempted to add more until you have let it rest for at least 20 minutes. Then taste again and add more if you think it needs it.
- Store in an airtight container in the fridge. The hummus should last 3–4 days.

Red Pepper and Chilli Hummus

400g chickpeas (you can use canned)

2–3 tablespoons olive oil or flax oil (great to get some omega into your diet)

Juice of ½ lemon

1 sweet red pepper

1 chilli, finely chopped

A dash of Tabasco sauce (optional – only if you like it very hot!)

2–4 cloves of garlic, depending on personal taste

1 tablespoon tahini paste (made from sesame seeds)

- Place all the ingredients into a blender and whizz until smooth. Add more lemon juice or olive oil until you get the desired consistency.
- If you taste this and think it is not garlicky enough, don't be tempted to add more until you have let it rest for at least 20 minutes. Then taste again and add more if you think it needs it.
- Store in an airtight container in the fridge. The hummus should last 3–4 days.

Lemon and Coriander Hummus

400g chickpeas (you can use canned)

2–3 tablespoons olive oil or flax oil (great to get some omega into your diet)

Juice and zest of 1 lemon

2–4 cloves of garlic, depending on personal taste

1 tablespoon tahini paste (made from sesame seeds)

A handful of fresh coriander leaves

- Place all the ingredients into a blender and whizz until smooth. Add more lemon juice or olive oil until you get the desired consistency.
- If you taste this and think it is not garlicky enough, don't be tempted to add more until you have let it rest for at least 20 minutes. Then taste again and add more if you think it needs it.
- Store in an airtight container in the fridge. The hummus should last 3–4 days.

Guacamole

Always use ripe avocados when making guacamole.

2 ripe avocados	1 onion, finely chopped
Juice of 1 lime	2 cloves of garlic, crushed
1 chilli, very finely chopped	1 ripe tomato, chopped (optional)

- Scoop out the flesh of the avocado and place in a bowl.
- Add the lime zest and juice, chilli, onion and garlic and stir well.
- If you are adding tomato, do this at the last minute, just prior to serving.

Tzatziki

½ cucumber, grated	125g natural yoghurt
2 cloves of garlic, crushed	

- Place the grated cucumber into a small bowl. Add the crushed garlic and natural yoghurt and blend well.
- Chill for 10–15 minutes before serving.

Spicy Coriander Dip

Juice of 1 lemon	1 small red onion
1 tablespoon olive oil	30g coconut
200g fresh coriander leaves	2.5cm (1in) knuckle of ginger
1 red chilli	1 tablespoon low fat crème fraiche

- Place all the ingredients in a blender and whizz until smooth.
- Leave to rest for 10 minutes before serving.

Salsa

A salsa is another gem to help use up any unwanted items lurking in your fridge. If you don't know what to do with the handful of tomatoes, end of a cucumber or those two spring onions that have slipped behind the salad drawer, this is for you. I was watching Jamie Oliver on TV one day and he was using up some fresh tomatoes. He made a salsa, but used the same recipe to mix with spaghetti for an instant dish with a bit of a kick. I now do this at home and it works brilliantly.

2–3 tomatoes, chopped	1–2 cloves of garlic, crushed
5–7.5cm (2–3in) of cucumber, diced	A dash of balsamic vinegar
1–2 chillies, finely chopped	A dash of olive oil
½ red pepper, finely chopped	A dash of lemon or lime juice
2–3 spring onions, finely chopped, including green stalks	Seasoning to taste

- Mix all the ingredients together in a bowl. Add more balsamic, olive oil or lemon/lime juice to taste.
- Leave to settle for at least 15 minutes to allow the flavours to infuse.

Note: You can add more chillies or even a splash of Tabasco sauce according to your taste. Some people add chopped apple or other vegetables they may have in the fridge. I always use fresh tomatoes as I prefer the flavour and it is also a great way to use up any ripe tomatoes. However, other people find tinned are perfectly acceptable.

Sour Cream and Chive

This is a great favourite, particularly with those who love dipping crisps or corn chips.

150g cream cheese	A dash of lemon juice
100ml sour cream	Seasoning to taste
A handful of chives, chopped	

- Place the cream cheese in a bowl and mix to soften. Add the sour cream and chives, with a little lemon juice if you prefer a creamier consistency.
- Season to taste.

One Pot Cakes and Desserts

Nearly everyone loves cakes and desserts and creating them is almost as much fun as eating them. Here are a few that can be prepared in 'one pot fashion' or baked in the slow cooker. Some are healthier than others, but all of them are delicious. You will find many more cake and dessert recipes in my book *Eat Well, Spend Less*.

Baked Lemon Cheesecake

Flan dish (ideally one with a removable bottom or spring

½ packet of digestive biscuits	Juice and zest of 1 lemon
50g butter	2 teaspoons vanilla essence
4 eggs	150ml double cream
500g cream cheese	A sprinkling of nutmeg
150g fine sugar	

- Preheat the oven to 180°C/gas mark 4.
- Place the biscuits in your food processor and whizz until they are reduced to crumbs. If you don't have a food processor, place them in a bag and crush gently with a wooden rolling pin until you have crumbs.
- Melt the butter in a saucepan. Stir in the biscuit crumbs ensuring they are evenly coated in butter.
- Spread over the base of your flan or pie dish.
- Separate the eggs. Place the whites in a bowl and beat until light and fluffy.
- In another bowl, mix the cream cheese, sugar, lemon and vanilla essence. When they are combined, add the egg yolks and cream and mix again.
- Carefully fold in the egg whites using a metal spoon until they are well combined. Pour over the biscuit base. Sprinkle generously with nutmeg.
- Bake in the oven for 40 minutes until firm. Remove from the oven and leave to cool before turning out of the tin and placing in the fridge to settle before serving.

Chocolate and Raspberry Pavlova

Mixer and baking tray

For the base
6 egg whites
300g sugar
50g cocoa powder, sifted
1 teaspoon white vinegar
50g dark chocolate (85% cocoa), grated

For the topping
400ml double cream
250g raspberries
25g dark chocolate (85% cocoa), grated

- Preheat the oven to 180°C/gas mark 4.
- Whip the egg whites in a mixer until fluffy, and then gradually add the sugar until you form a firm meringue.
- Sprinkle the cocoa, vinegar and chocolate on top of the meringue and fold in.
- Spread over a lined baking tray to form a circle about 4–5cm (1½–2in) thick or more. Smooth over with a spatula.
- Turn down the oven to 150°C/gas mark 2 and bake for 1–1½ hours. The meringue should be firm and dry around the edges and top but slightly squidgy in the centre.
- Remove from the oven and allow to cool.
- Meanwhile whip the cream for the topping. (For extra decadence, add a tablespoon of liqueur to the whipped cream.)
- When the meringue is cool, spoon the cream on top and cover with raspberries. Enjoy!

Chocolate Mousse Cake

This is a really yummy dessert that will impress your family and friends, but be warned – it is very rich. A little goes a long way, so stick to modest-sized portions!

Saucepan and pie dish (ideally one with a removable bottom or spring)

For the base
½ packet of digestive biscuits
50g butter

For the topping
50g butter
50g mini marshmallows
75g plain chocolate
50ml orange juice
I teaspoon vanilla extract
250ml double cream

- Place the biscuits in your food processor and whizz until they are reduced to crumbs. If you don't have a food processor, place them in a bag and crush gently with a wooden rolling pin until you have crumbs.
- Melt the butter in a saucepan. Stir in the biscuit crumbs ensuring they are evenly coated in the butter. Spread over the base of your flan or pie dish.
- Chill the biscuit base in the fridge while you make the topping.
- In a saucepan, gently melt the butter, marshmallows, chocolate and orange juice. When they are melted, add the vanilla extract.
- Meanwhile whip the double cream to soft – not hard – whip.
- Leave the marshmallow and chocolate mixture to cool and then add to the whipped cream. Fold in carefully. If the mixture curdles, don't worry, keep mixing and it will correct itself.
- Pour this onto the biscuit base and leave to set.
- You can decorate the cake with more whipped cream or simply cover it with a dusting of cocoa or icing sugar. At Christmas you could make a star or Christmas tree template to place over the flan before sprinkling with icing sugar.

Lemon Meringue Pie

This was my brother's favourite when we were growing up – oh, the memories come flooding back (especially as I often wanted to aim one at his head)!

Saucepan and pie dish

For the lemon filling
200g caster sugar
50g cornflour
350ml water
Juice and zest of 2 lemons
25g butter
4 egg yolks

For the meringue topping
4 egg whites
75g caster sugar

- Preheat the oven 180°C/gas mark 4.
- You should have your pastry case, cooked and cooled, ready for use.
- In a saucepan, combine the sugar, cornflour, water, lemon juice and zest. Heat slowly and gently, taking care not to let the mixture burn. When it is just below simmering, add the butter.
- Separate the eggs into two bowls. Beat the yolks and add a couple of spoonfuls of the cornflour mixture, then pour this back into the cornflour mix.
- Cook slowly until the mixture starts to thicken, then remove from the heat. You can now pour this into the pastry case.
- While the filling is cooling, prepare the meringue. Beat the egg whites until foaming and light. Add the sugar and continue to whip until the mixture forms peaks – you should be able to turn the bowl upside down and the meringue remains inside.
- Spread the meringue over the filling, making sure you cover the edges well to help seal the flan.
- Bake for 10–15 minutes, until the meringue is golden.
- Serve hot or cold.

Steamed Raisin and Apple Pudding

Slow cooker or steamer

75g butter	100g raisins
75g brown sugar	2 cooking apples, diced
Zest of 1 lemon	2 teaspoons ground cinnamon
2 eggs	A generous grating of nutmeg
150g self-raising flour	

- Cream the butter and sugar together in a mixing bowl. Add the eggs, beat well and follow with the sifted flour and lemon zest.
- Add the raisins, apples, cinnamon and nutmeg. Stir well.
- Spoon the mixture into a greased 1 litre pudding basin.
- Cover with greaseproof paper, followed by two layers of tinfoil. Tie firmly with string to secure.
- Steam in a steamer for 1½ hours. Alternatively, place in a slow cooker. Fill the cooker with enough warm water to reach halfway up the sides of the pudding basin. Turn the cooker to high and cook for 2–3 hours.
- Serve with home-made custard or a dollop of crème fraiche.

Key Lime Pie

You can make this by simply mixing two cans of condensed milk with your limes, but I have opted for a slightly lower fat option, but with all the great taste. If you don't like limes, you can use lemons for a great zesty dessert.

Mixing bowl and flan dish

For the base
150g digestive biscuits
60g butter

For the filling
Zest and juice of 3 limes
400ml can of light condensed milk
125ml Greek yoghurt (I use Total 0%)
150ml extra thick double cream (or you can use thick low fat crème fraiche)

- Place the biscuits in your food processor and whizz until they are reduced to crumbs. If you don't have a food processor, place them in a bag and crush gently with a wooden rolling pin until you have crumbs.
- Melt the butter in a saucepan. Stir in the biscuit crumbs ensuring they are evenly coated in the butter.
- Spread over the base of a 17.5cm (7in) flan or pie dish and press down firmly. Leave in the fridge to cool while you make the filling.
- Remove the zest from the limes before juicing. Mix the lime zest, juice and condensed milk together thoroughly. Add the yoghurt and cream or crème fraiche and stir well.
- Pour this mixture over the biscuit base. Return to the fridge to set.
- Before serving you can decorate with swirls of grated dark chocolate.

Egg Custard

When I was a child I wouldn't drink milk so my mum used to make me milky puddings. To this day egg custard remains a favourite of mine, especially if I am feeling under the weather or need a metaphorical hug!

Ovenproof dish or slow cooker

4 eggs	30g sugar
I teaspoon cornflour	I teaspoon vanilla extract
500ml milk	Freshly grated nutmeg

To make the custard

- Beat the eggs. Mix the cornflour with a little of the milk to form a smooth paste. Pour this onto the eggs with the remainder of the milk and beat the mixture – but take care not to over beat. Add the sugar and vanilla extract and combine well.
- Pour into the ovenproof dish. Grate a little fresh nutmeg over the top of the pudding.

To cook in the oven

- Preheat the oven to 170°C/gas mark 3.
- Place the ovenproof dish in a roasting tray. Fill the roasting tray with water to create a bain-marie.
- Cook in the oven for 35–45 minutes, until the custard is firm to the touch, but may still have a slight wobble (but is not runny).

To cook in a slow cooker

- Preheat your slow cooker if necessary according to the manufacturer's instructions.
- Make sure your ovenproof dish fits in your slow cooker.
- Cover the dish with tinfoil and ensure it is well sealed.
- Place the dish in the slow cooker. Fill the cooker with enough warm water to come halfway up the sides of the ovenproof dish.
- Turn the cooker to high and cook for 2–3 hours, until the custard is firm.

Note: You can cook these in mini ramekin dishes and make individual puddings. Decorate with raspberries for some added colour and zing.

Individual Slow Cook Blackberry and Apple Upside-down Cake

Slow cooker

For the cake mixture	**For the blackberry and apple mixture**
100g butter	50g butter
100g sugar	50g brown sugar
2 eggs	1–2 Bramley apples, chopped
1 teaspoon vanilla extract	30–50g blackberries
100g self-raising flour, sieved	

- Place the butter and sugar in a mixer and beat until light and fluffy. Gradually add the eggs and vanilla extract. Fold in the sieved flour.
- Grease 4–6 ramekin dishes or similar-sized non-stick pots. I normally coat them with butter then sprinkle over flour to form a seal.
- To make the blackberry and apple mixture, gently melt the butter and brown sugar over a low heat. Place some apple and blackberries in the base of each dish. Pour over the butter/brown sugar syrup – a little in each dish.
- Top with the cake mixture. You can add more apple or blackberries to the cake mixture if you like, or just add a few pieces to the top of the cakes. Sprinkle with a touch of brown sugar.
- Place in a slow cooker and cook for 2 hours, or until the sponge is firm to the touch. Carefully remove the cakes from the slow cooker, taking care not to burn yourself as the dishes will be very hot.
- To serve, carefully loosen the sides of the cakes. Place a plate over the top of the dishes (top side of the plate meeting the top of the dishes as you are turning these out onto the plate). Hold the plate firmly onto the dish and flip over. The cake should come away easily and sit on the plate, apple and blackberry side up. Finish with a dollop of cream, crème fraiche or ice-cream. Delicious.

Note: If using a crockery slow cooker, place on trivet and fill halfway up the sides of the dish with water.

Banana and Home-made Custard

This was a huge favourite when we were kids. This recipe is for home-made custard, but if you want to cheat you can buy ready-made. I use full fat milk as it gives a creamier taste and avoids having to use cream but, if you prefer, you can used semi-skimmed.

Saucepan

600ml full fat milk	3 tablespoons sugar
4 egg yolks	1 teaspoon vanilla essence
4 tablespoons cornflour	2–3 bananas

- Heat the milk until just below boiling point. While it is heating up, mix the egg yolks, cornflour, sugar and vanilla essence together. Be careful to keep an eye on the milk to make sure it doesn't boil over.
- Remove the milk from the heat and add the egg mixture. Use a hand whisk and stir well.
- Return to the heat and continue to stir until the custard starts to thicken – take care not to have the heat too high or the mixture will burn.
- Once it has reached your desired thickness remove from the heat. Chop your bananas and add to the custard. Serve immediately.

Note: If you have any custard left over, pour it into lolly moulds and freeze – it makes delicious ice lollies!

Apple and Walnut Loaf

Apple cakes of any description are a great favourite of mine. The flavour of apple combined with cinnamon is delicious. Thankfully, my husband agrees, so does not mind me cooking apple cakes on a regular basis – shame about my waistline though!

Oven bake or slow cooker

100g butter

150g sugar

2 eggs, beaten

200g self-raising flour, sifted

2 teaspoons cinnamon powder

2 cooking apples, chopped

50g chopped walnuts

To cook in the oven

- Preheat the oven to 180°C/gas mark 4.
- Mix the butter and sugar together until light and fluffy.
- Add the eggs a little at a time, continuing to mix well.
- Add the sifted flour and cinnamon powder and combine until thoroughly mixed.
- Add the chopped apple and walnuts. When thoroughly combined, spoon the mixture into a lined or greased 1kg (2lb) loaf tin.
- Bake in the oven for 50–60 minutes, until a skewer or knife inserted into the centre of the cake comes out clean.
- Cool on a cooling rack before storing in an airtight container.

To cook in a slow cooker

- To make the cake, follow steps 2–5 for the oven method, above. Make sure you use a solid cake tin, not one with a loose bottom. Cover the tin with foil, making sure it is secure.
- To cook the cake, you have two options. You can place the tin in the slow cooker on a trivet or upturned saucer, pour in boiling water around the sides of the tin, ensuring the water reaches no higher than halfway up the tin, and cook for 4–6 hours on low. Alternatively, you can place the tin directly in the slow cooker, add the water as above and cook on high for 2–3 hours, or until the cake is firm in the centre. I have tried both methods and prefer to place the tin directly in the slow cooker. I have had no problems except that on one occasion the greaseproof paper at the bottom of the tin was a bit burnt. Other than that, everything was fine.
- Cool on a cooling rack before storing in an airtight container.

Rhubarb and Orange Layer

I found this recipe in an old family notebook, where it was called an orange and rhubarb raver. I'm not sure what the raver bit is, but I tried the recipe and my husband loved it. So, here goes – I hope you like it too.

Ovenproof dish

600g rhubarb, cut into chunks

2 oranges, finely sliced (peeled or unpeeled)

2 level teaspoons redcurrant jelly

50g butter

50g brown sugar

2 tablespoons golden syrup

50g porridge oats

50g granola

- Preheat the oven to 180°C/gas mark 4.
- Wash and slice the rhubarb into chunks. Thinly slice the oranges, and then cut each slice in half.
- Place the rhubarb and orange slices in an ovenproof dish, making sure they are evenly distributed. Carefully spread or dollop the redcurrant jelly over the rhubarb.
- In a saucepan, melt the butter, followed by the sugar and golden syrup. Once they are melted, add the oats and granola and cook for 2–3 minutes.
- Spread the oat mixture on top of the rhubarb and oranges. Once they are covered, press down gently.
- Bake in the oven for 35–45 minutes, until the top is golden brown.
- Serve with a generous dollop of crème fraiche or ice cream.

Semolina Pudding

Makes you think about school dinners, doesn't it? Don't let that put you off, though; cooked well, this can be a really comforting pudding. If all else fails, keep the dried semolina in your store cupboard to sprinkle onto your roast potatoes!

Saucepan and ovenproof dish

600ml milk	I egg yolk
50g semolina	Zest of I orange
50g sugar	50ml single cream
I teaspoon vanilla extract	A sprinkling of grated nutmeg

- Preheat the oven to 180°C/gas mark 4.
- Heat the milk in a saucepan until it is almost boiling. Add the semolina and sugar and stir until the mixture starts to thicken.
- Once it has thickened, remove from the heat and stir in all the remaining ingredients.
- Pour into a greased ovenproof dish. Sprinkle with grated nutmeg and bake in the oven for 15 minutes.

Carrot Cake

This has been successfully cooked in the slow cooker as well as in the oven, so experiment to see which texture you prefer.

Oven or slow cooker

400g self-raising flour

2 teaspoons cinnamon

1 teaspoon ground coriander

½ teaspoon grated nutmeg

150g brown sugar

80ml light vegetable oil

60ml water

2 eggs, beaten

200g carrots, grated

60g sultanas

30g desiccated coconut

To cook in the oven

• Preheat the oven to 180°C/gas mark 4.

• Place the dry ingredients (except the coconut) in your mixer. In a separate bowl or jug, mix the oil, water and eggs together. They only need to be roughly mixed, so don't worry if they stay separated!

• Pour into the dry mixture and whizz to form a batter. Add the grated carrots, sultanas and coconut.

• Mix well. Pour into a greased cake tin.

• Bake in the oven for 45–55 minutes until firm to the touch and a skewer inserted into the centre of the cake comes out clean.

To cook in a slow cooker

• To make the cake, follow steps 2–4 for the oven method, above.

• To cook the cake, you have two options. You can place the tin in the slow cooker on a trivet or upturned saucer, pour in boiling water around the sides of the tin, ensuring the water reaches no higher than halfway up the tin, and cook for 4–6 hours on low. Alternatively, you can place the tin directly in the slow cooker, add the water as above and cook on high for 2–3 hours, or until the cake is firm in the centre. I have tried both methods and prefer to place the tin directly in the slow cooker. I have had no problems except that on one occasion the greaseproof paper at the bottom of the tin was a bit burnt. Other than that, everything was fine.

• Cool on cooling rack before storing in airtight container.

Blackberry Layer Sponge Pudding

Steamer or slow cooker

100g butter	150g self-raising flour, sifted
100g sugar	1 teaspoon vanilla extract
2 eggs	200g blackberries

- Beat the butter and the sugar together until golden. Gradually add the eggs – if the mixture starts to curdle, add a touch of the flour.
- Add the flour and continue to beat well.
- Mix in the vanilla extract.
- Grease a 1 litre (2 pint) pudding basin. Place a couple of spoonfuls of the sponge mix into the basin. Sprinkle in a few blackberries, add more sponge mix and continue layering until you reach the top of the bowl. Finish with a layer of sponge mix.
- Cover with baking parchment and two layers of tinfoil. Tie securely with string.

To cook in a steamer
- Cook in the steamer for 1½ hours. Make sure you check the water level regularly and top it up if necessary.
- Serve with home-made custard or crème fraiche.

To cook in a slow cooker
- Place the basin in the slow cooker. Add enough warm water to come halfway up the outside of the basin.
- Turn the cooker to high and cook for 3–4 hours, or until the pudding is firm to the touch.
- Serve with home-made custard or crème fraiche.

Winter Fruit Compote

This makes a wonderful dessert, or a warm breakfast, either on its own or as an accompaniment to home-made porridge.

Saucepan or slow cooker

100g prunes	1 cinnamon stick
100g figs	4–6 whole cloves
50g currants	2 oranges, peeled and sliced
50g raisins	Zest and juice of 1 orange
350ml water	1 banana, sliced
1 tablespoon brown sugar	

• Place the dried fruit in a saucepan with the water, sugar, cinnamon and cloves. Bring to the boil.
• Add the sliced oranges, orange zest and juice. Cover and cook on a low/medium heat for 15–20 minutes, adding more water if necessary. Remove the cinnamon stick and cloves.
• Add the sliced banana just prior to serving.

Note: If you want to make this in a slow cooker, set it to low and cook for 4–6 hours. Add the banana half an hour before serving; if you add it earlier it will just turn to a brown mush.

Orange and Grand Marnier Syllabub

Mixing bowl and serving dishes

Zest and juice of 2 oranges	50g caster sugar
4 tablespoons Grand Marnier	450ml double cream

• Mix the zest and juice of the oranges together. Add the Grand Marnier, caster sugar and cream and whip together.
• Place a small amount in shot glasses or small serving dishes. You can decorate with fruit or a biscuit.

Crock-Pot Christmas Pudding

This recipe was kindly given to me by Crock-Pot. It is the perfect Christmas pudding recipe to make in your slow cooker.

Mixing bowl and slow cooker

75g plain flour	100g fresh white breadcrumbs
½ teaspoon ground nutmeg	50g mixed peel
¼ teaspoon mixed spice	1 small cooking apple, grated
75g suet	Grated zest and juice of 1 lemon
150g dark brown sugar	2 eggs, beaten
150g currants	2 tablespoons brandy
125g raisins	
125g sultanas	Baking paper, foil and string
25g almonds, roughly chopped	

- Grease a 1.2 litre (2 pint) pudding basin.
- Sift together the flour, nutmeg and mixed spice into a bowl.
- Add the suet, brown sugar, dried fruit, almonds, breadcrumbs and peel. Mix well.
- Add the apple, lemon zest and juice, eggs and brandy. Stir well until all the ingredients are well combined.
- Pour into the pudding basin and cover with a greased round of baking parchment.
- Take a square of foil, larger than the top of the basin; make a pleat in the centre to allow for any expansion during cooking.
- Place over the basin and seal well with string, making sure it is tight. It is advisable to make a handle with the string to enable you to remove the basin from the hot pan in the slow cooker.
- Place the pudding in the stoneware and pour enough boiling water to come three-quarters of the way up the basin. Cook for 8–10 hours on low; the longer the cooking time, the darker the pudding will be.
- To reheat the pudding, place in the stoneware with boiling water and reheat on high for 3 hours.

Note: The pudding may be made a few months before Christmas, stored in a cool, dark place and occasionally fed with brandy.

Fresh Fruit Salad

This is a very quick and easy option for a healthy but sumptuous dessert. There are no hard and fast rules – raid your fruit bowl and fridge to put together a zesty dessert to suit you and your family.

Serving bowl

Apples	Melon
Oranges	Grapes
Pears	Pineapple
Raspberries	Nectarine
Strawberries	Peach
Banana	Orange juice

- Chop your chosen fruit into bite-size pieces. Pour orange juice (or any juice of your choice) over the fruit.
- Leave to settle for 10–20 minutes before serving.

Apple and Cinnamon Cobbler

Ovenproof dish

4–6 Bramley cooking apples, sliced	150g self-raising flour, sifted
1–2 tablespoons brown sugar (depending on desired sweetness)	½ teaspoon baking powder
Juice of ½ lemon	25g sugar
1–2 teaspoons ground cinnamon	50g butter
50g raisins	100ml natural yoghurt
	1 teaspoon vanilla essence

- Preheat the oven to 200°C/gas mark 6.
- Place the apples, sugar, lemon juice, cinnamon and raisins in a saucepan. Add 30ml of water. Cook on a medium heat until the apples start to soften, but still retain some firmness.
- Meanwhile, place the flour, baking powder and sugar in a bowl. Rub the butter into the flour until the mixture resembles breadcrumbs.
- Add the yoghurt and vanilla essence and mix thoroughly to form a dough.
- Place the dough on a floured surface and roll into a thick sausage. Cut into 2.5–5cm (1–2in) pieces to make scones.
- Pour the apple mixture into an ovenproof dish. Place the scones around the edges and over the top of the apple mixture and coat with a little milk and a sprinkling of brown sugar. Bake in the oven for 12–15 minutes.

Creamy Raspberry Bread-and-butter Pudding

Ovenproof dish or slow cooker

Butter	2 eggs
6–8 slices of bread (stale is perfect for this pudding)	1 teaspoon vanilla essence
	Brown sugar
300ml milk	150g raspberries

To cook in the oven
- Preheat the oven to 180°C/gas mark 4.
- Grease the ovenproof dish with butter to prevent the pudding from sticking.
- Butter the bread slices (it's entirely up to you whether or not you remove the crusts). Mix the milk, eggs and vanilla essence together.
- Put a layer of bread in the dish, butter side up, followed by a layer of raspberries and sprinkle over some sugar. Continue with alternate layers of bread, fruit and sugar. Finally, pour over the milk mixture.
- Bake in the oven for 20–30 minutes, until golden.
- Serve with a generous dollop of crème fraiche.

To cook in a slow cooker
- To make the pudding, follow steps 2–4 for the oven method, above.
- Check that your ovenproof dish fits in the slow cooker. Cover the bread-and-butter pudding with foil, making sure it is secure. Pour hot water into the slow cooker, so that it comes no higher than halfway up the sides of the pudding dish. Turn the cooker to high and cook for 4–6 hours.
- Serve with a generous dollop of crème fraiche.

Baked Honeyed Figs

This is a wonderful dish to make when fresh figs are in season. Serve with some crème fraiche or ice cream – delicious.

Ovenproof dish

6–8 figs	Brown sugar
Honey	Sliced almonds

- Preheat the oven to 150°C/gas mark 2 (or you can put these in a hot oven that has just been turned off – they will cook gently while you eat your main meal).
- Place the figs on a greased ovenproof dish. Drizzle with honey and sprinkle with brown sugar. Sprinkle over some sliced almonds.
- Place in a low oven for 10–15 minutes. The oven temperature needs to be low so that the sugar doesn't burn.
- Serve with a generous dollop of crème fraiche or ice cream. Yummy!

Ginger and Lemon Twist

This is a really simple dessert that looks fabulous when served in glasses. It takes minutes to make and tastes divine!

Mixing bowl and serving glasses

12–15 ginger biscuits, crushed	Zest and juice of 1 lemon
250g Greek yoghurt	½ jar of lemon curd
100g low fat cream cheese	

- Crush the ginger biscuits and place a small amount in the bottom of each serving glass.
- Mix the yoghurt and cream cheese together until smooth. Add the zest and juice of the lemon. Mix thoroughly.
- Carefully fold in the lemon curd, creating a twisted ripple. Spoon into the glasses and leave in the fridge for at least 30 minutes before serving.

Hot Chocolate Brownie Pudding

This is one of our family's favourites. You can serve it hot, which is really divine, or cold with a nice cup of tea. Whatever you choose, one thing is for certain – it won't be around for long!

Food mixer and baking tray

225g self-raising flour

200g brown sugar

100g plain cocoa powder

350ml water (or orange juice if you like chocolate orange flavour)

200ml light vegetable oil

1 teaspoon vanilla extract

50g plain chocolate chips

25g white chocolate chips (optional)

15g grated cacao chocolate (optional – gives extra dark chocolate zing)

- Preheat the oven to 180°C/gas mark 4.
- In a large bowl, stir together the dry ingredients.
- Add the water, vegetable oil and vanilla extract. Whisk until thoroughly mixed.
- Add the chocolate chips and the cacao, if you are using it. Pour into a lined or greased baking tray.
- Bake for 25–30 minutes. Leave in the tray for 10 minutes before turning onto a cooling rack and cutting into squares.
- Serve warm with a dollop of crème fraiche or rich chocolate sauce for a naughty but very nice dessert!

Bread-and-butter Pudding

I have not included weights in this recipe, purely as it would be too fussy to weigh out ingredients when all you need to do is add a sprinkle and layer accordingly. If you want to add variety, you could use other dried fruit such as apricots or even cranberries.

Ovenproof dish or slow cooker

6–8 slices of bread (you can use slightly stale bread)
Butter
Desiccated coconut
Raisins
Brown sugar

2 teaspoons cornflour
500–650ml milk
Vanilla essence
Nutmeg
Cinnamon

To cook in the oven
- Preheat the oven 180°C/gas mark 4.
- Grease the ovenproof dish with butter to prevent the pudding from sticking.
- Butter the bread slices and place one layer in the bottom of the dish. Sprinkle with coconut, raisins and brown sugar. Continue layering until the dish is complete.
- Mix the cornflour, milk, vanilla essence, nutmeg and cinnamon together. Pour over the bread mixture and leave to settle for 15 minutes before placing in the oven.
- Bake for 30–40 minutes, until golden. Serve with crème fraiche.

To cook in a slow cooker
- To make the pudding, follow steps 2–4 for the oven method, above.
- Check that your ovenproof dish fits in the slow cooker. Cover the bread-and-butter pudding with foil, making sure it is secure. Pour hot water into the slow cooker, so that it comes no higher than halfway up the sides of the pudding dish. Turn the cooker to medium/high and cook for 4–6 hours. Serve with crème fraiche.

No Messing Rice Pudding

Most people cook rice pudding in the oven, but I find making it in a saucepan so much easier. I have also prepared it in a slow cooker – though don't do this in a crockery slow cooker as you may find the flavour of garlic from your savoury dishes will taint your pudding – yuck!

I make this with soya milk as I prefer not to have too much dairy produce, but you can use any milk you like. Full fat adds creaminess, or stir in some double cream prior to serving. If you want to use soya milk, try stirring in some Alpro soya alternative to cream – surprisingly, it gives the same result as cream.

Saucepan or slow cooker

75g pudding rice or Arborio risotto rice	1–2 teaspoons pure vanilla extract
1 litre of milk (see above)	25g sugar
2–3 teaspoons cinnamon	

- Place all the ingredients into a heavy-based pan or slow cooker – make sure this pan is at least a third larger in volume than the contents.
- Cook the rice on a low heat until soft, stirring occasionally to avoid the rice sticking to the base of your pan. The rice will thicken and you may have to add more liquid. This should take 20–30 minutes on a hob, or 4–6 hours on low setting if you are using a slow cooker.
- Prior to serving, you can stir in some cream (see above) if you like a creamy taste. Spoon the pudding into bowls and sprinkle with nutmeg.

Note: My family love a **Raspberry Rice Pudding Brûlée**. I place some frozen raspberries in the base of an ovenproof dish (or mini ramekin dishes), add rice pudding and finish with a sprinkle of brown sugar. I then use my cook's blow torch to caramelise the top (you can get a similar effect by placing under the grill but it does take longer). This also works with other leftover fruit. Another favourite is **Rhubarb and Ginger Rice Pudding Brûlée**. Using the same technique as above, place rhubarb chunks in the base of the ramekins or ovenproof dish. Add a sprinkle of fresh grated ginger to the rhubarb – be careful as it can give quite a kick! Cover with rice pudding and sprinkle with brown sugar before caramelising as above. Delicious!

Simple Baked Apples

This is a deliciously simple autumnal pudding that always leaves people satisfied. You can stuff the apples with whatever you fancy, but I tend to cheat and add a generous dollop of mincemeat or, if there is none in the store cupboard, I will fill them with a mixture of dried fruit and a sprinkle of brown sugar.

Ovenproof dish

---

4 Bramley apples, cored but not peeled
Mincemeat, or mixed dried fruit

Brown sugar

- Preheat the oven to 180°C/gas mark 4.
- Wash and core your apples, leaving the skins intact.
- Place the apples on a baking tray or ovenproof dish.
- Fill the empty cores with mincemeat or dried fruit. Finish with a sprinkling of brown sugar.
- Bake in the oven for 30–40 minutes until soft.
- Serve with low fat crème fraiche or natural yoghurt.

Note: In early September, try to make use of the plump ripe blackberries in the hedgerows, and fill the apple cores with these delicious bulging berries to make **Baked Blackberry Apples**. Place these in an ovenproof dish as you will get plenty of sticky juice oozing out from the apples.

Blackberry and Apple Cobbler

Ovenproof dish or slow cooker

For the blackberry and apple mixture
4 cooking apples (ideally, Bramley), sliced
1 or 2 handfuls of blackberries (fresh or
   frozen)
25g brown sugar

For the cobbler topping
150g self-raising flour
25g sugar
50g butter
100ml natural yoghurt
1 teaspoon vanilla essence

To cook in the oven
• Preheat the oven to 180°C/gas mark 4.
• Place the apples in a saucepan or ovenproof dish with 1–2 tablespoons of water. Cook on
  medium heat for 5–8 minutes until the apples start to soften but most remain firm.
• Mix in the blackberries and brown sugar. Stir well.
• Pour into an ovenproof dish.
• To make the scone mix, place the flour and sugar in a bowl and rub in the butter. Add the
  yoghurt and vanilla essence and mix to form a dough. If this is too dry, add a touch of
  milk. Place on a floured board and roll out to about 2–4cm (1–1½in) thick. Cut into
  scone shapes. Place on the top of the blackberry and apple mixture and brush with milk.
• Bake in the oven for 15–20 minutes.

To cook in a slow cooker
• To make the cobbler, follow steps 2–5 for the oven method, above. Check that your
  ovenproof dish fits in the slow cooker. Cover the cobbler with foil, making sure it is
  secure. Pour hot water in the slow cooker, so that it comes no higher than halfway up the
  sides of the cobbler dish.
• Turn the cooker to medium/high and cook for 3–4 hours until the scones are light and
  fluffy.

Variations
There are endless combinations for a good fruit cobbler. Go with the seasons and try to use
up any spare fruit in your fruit bowl. Here are some more ideas:

Spiced Apple Cobbler – after stewing the apple, stir in some nutmeg, cinnamon and mixed spice with a handful of dried fruit.

Apple and Blackcurrant Cobbler – just like blackberries, blackcurrants add a wonderful flavour and vibrant colour to your cobbler. Place the blackcurrants in the saucepan with the apple to stew together before pouring the fruit into the ovenproof dish and adding your topping.

Apple and Blueberry Cobbler – blueberries are marketed as a superfood, but really all berries are good for you. Mix fresh or frozen blueberries into the stewed apple before placing in an ovenproof dish and covering in your topping.

Simple Gooseberry Fool

Gooseberry fools are lovely, but they can be high in fat, especially when made with full fat cream. I use Total Greek Yoghurt as it is low fat and holds its thickness. I suppose really this is gooseberry yoghurt. For those who would like a creamy fool, you can supplement cream for half the yoghurt. Buy your gooseberries in season or grow your own.

Saucepan and serving glasses

400g gooseberries
50g sugar
250g Total Greek Yoghurt

- Place the gooseberries in a pan with the sugar and gently cook until the gooseberries pop when pushed with a spoon.
- Leave the gooseberries to cool and then fold in the yoghurt.
- Place in serving dishes to set.
- This is delicious served with ginger biscuit crumbs sprinkled on the top.

Note: You can make **Rhubarb Fools** by following the same process. If you have a very sweet tooth you may want to add more sugar.

Chocolate Fondue

Fondues are a quick and easy dessert to make for dinner parties and guarantee good conversation. They are also a great way to get some fresh fruit into your children. OK, we are coating the fruit in chocolate, but if you use dark organic chocolate you will avoid unnecessary sugar hits and hopefully educate your children in the delights of great dark chocolate instead of the inferior sugary, milky confectionery.

200g dark chocolate	A selection of fresh fruit, chopped

- If you have a fondue set, this is easy – simply melt the chocolate in your bain- marie (otherwise known as a double boiler, where you place water in the bottom pan and the chocolate in the top pan. The heat of the water boiling melts the chocolate.)
- Transfer the chocolate to your fondue set. If you don't have a fondue set, keep the chocolate over the bain-marie as it will stay warm for approximately 10 minutes.
- While the chocolate is melting, place the fruit on a platter ready for dipping.
- Simply dip your chosen fruit into the chocolate and enjoy!

Note: Why not offer some sweet dips alongside the chocolate? Try fruit yoghurt; crème fraiche mixed with crushed strawberries; cream cheese mixed with lemon zest, juice and a spoonful of cream; or try a sweet dressing made from fruit juice, sweetened with honey.

Baked Peach and Almond Delights

Just like baked apples, this is a very simple dish but tastes wonderful. You can add a touch of luxury by drizzling a dash of Cointreau, or whichever is your favourite liqueur, over the peaches just before adding the yoghurt mixture. Remember, as with most fruit and vegetables, it is cheaper, and better environmentally, to buy them when they are in season.

Ovenproof dish

4 ripe peaches, halved and stoned	**For the topping**
4 teaspoons honey	100ml natural yoghurt
18–24 raspberries (you can use frozen or, if you have no raspberries, raspberry jam – but omit the honey!)	100ml quark
	1 teaspoon honey
	Zest of 1 orange
75g flaked almonds	1 teaspoon vanilla essence

- Preheat the oven to 180°C/gas mark 4.
- Place the halved and stoned peaches in an ovenproof tray, flesh facing upwards.
- In the centre of each peach half, where the stone was, add ½ teaspoon of honey and top with 2–3 raspberries.
- Sprinkle the flaked almonds over the top of the peaches, retaining a few almonds for later.
- Bake in the oven for 15 minutes.
- Meanwhile, mix the yoghurt, quark, honey, orange zest and vanilla essence together.
- When the peaches are ready, place them in serving bowls with a dollop of the yoghurt mixture. Sprinkle with the remaining almonds before serving.

Crème Brûlée

I shamelessly pinched this recipe from a blog – it's really great, so I had to include it here. It is such a simple dish to make in the slow cooker, requiring very little effort on your part. I hope you enjoy it!

Slow cooker

450ml double cream

5 egg yolks

110g fine sugar

1 tablespoon vanilla extract

55g brown sugar (for topping only)

- Select an ovenproof dish that fits comfortably within your slow cooker. Turn your slow cooker to hot.
- Pour hot water around the dish so that it comes halfway up the outside – acting as a bain-marie.
- In a mixing bowl, whip all the ingredients together, apart from the brown sugar, which is used for the topping. Pour this mixture into the ovenproof dish. Cover with buttered tin foil and cook on high for 2–4 hours. The custard should start to set in the centre but may be slightly loose around the edges.
- Remove the crème brûlée carefully – it will be hot!
- Leave to cool completely before placing in the fridge for 2–3 hours.
- Prior to serving, sprinkle with brown sugar and use a kitchen blow torch to brown/caramelise the sugar. You can use a grill for this but it is not so easy. Leave to chill for 5–10 minutes before serving.

Steamed Lemon Pudding

Slow cooker

125g butter	1 teaspoon vanilla extract
125g sugar	125g self-raising flour
2 eggs	50g sugar
Zest and juice of 2 lemons	

- Preheat your slow cooker according to the manufacturer's instructions.
- Beat the butter and 125g sugar together until pale and creamy. Add the eggs and beat until smooth.
- Grate the lemon zest into the batter mix. Add the vanilla extract. Stir in the flour and combine until smooth.
- Juice the lemons and mix this with the remaining 50g sugar.
- Thoroughly grease a 1 litre (2 pint) pudding basin. Pour the lemon and sugar mixture into the bottom of the basin.
- Top with the sponge mix. Cover with a layer of baking parchment followed by two layers of tinfoil. Tie securely with string.
- Place the basin in the slow cooker. Pour warm water into the slow cooker until it comes halfway up the sides of the pudding basin. Turn the cooker to high and cook for 3 hours, or until firm.
- Turn out the pudding onto a plate, allowing the lemon juice to seep over the sponge. Serve with home-made custard or crème fraiche.

Hot Chocolate Orange Brownie Mugs

A friend of mine made these and they were a big hit with everyone. They really are a hug in a mug.

Slow cooker

110g self-raising flour	1 teaspoon orange essence (optional)
100g brown sugar	1 teaspoon vanilla essence
75g cocoa	25g dark chocolate chips
100ml oil	A spray of olive oil
150ml orange juice	4–6 ovenproof mugs

- Preheat the slow cooker according to the manufacturer's instructions.
- To prepare the brownie mix, put all the dry ingredients into your food mixer. Measure the oil and orange juice and mix together with the orange and vanilla essences (or you can use the zest of 1 orange instead of orange essence).
- Pour this into the dried mix and beat well until thoroughly mixed.
- Stir in by hand the chocolate chips, ensuring they are evenly distributed.
- Carefully spray the insides of the mugs with oil (or you can rub them with butter, and then sprinkle on flour to form a non-stick base).
- Fill the mugs half-full with the mixture.
- Turn the slow cooker to high. Carefully place the mugs in the slow cooker on a trivet. These should be fine in your stoneware pot as long as the mugs are dishwasher and microwave proof. Normally the chunkier mugs are suitable – not fine bone china! Pour in boiling water around the sides of the mugs, ensuring the water reaches no higher than halfway up the mugs. Alternatively, you can place the mugs directly in the slow cooker and add the water as above
- Cook for 2 hours or until the brownies have risen and are firm to the touch.
- Very carefully remove the mugs from the slow cooker – use oven gloves for this. Hold the mugs at the top and run the handles under cold water. This will cool them enough for you to be able to hold them.
- If you like you can decorate the brownies with cream or crème fraiche before serving.

Eton Mess

This can be made in minutes and is always a wonderful dessert. You can make your own meringues but in this recipe I am using shop bought. I like to have these ingredients in my store cupboard, ready for when we have a sweet craving!

4–6 meringue nests, broken into pieces
350g raspberries

½ bottle of raspberry sauce/coulis
300ml double cream

- Gather together your ingredients. If you are using frozen raspberries (which are ideal for this as it doesn't matter if they are not perfectly formed), make sure they are defrosted. I use raspberry sauce (available from supermarkets) as this enhances the flavour, but this is optional.
- Whip the double cream until it is light and fluffy but not too thick.
- In individual dishes, or one large serving dish, layer the meringue, raspberry sauce, raspberries and double cream, in any order.
- Serve and enjoy!

Banoffee Pie

Saucepan and flan tin

Cooked pastry case or flan base
150g butter
30g brown sugar
400g tin of sweet condensed milk

2–3 bananas, sliced
200ml double cream
A little plain chocolate, grated, to garnish

- If you have not already done this, you will need to blind bake your pastry in a flan dish, or you can cheat and buy ready-cooked pastry cases.
- In a saucepan, melt the butter, sugar and condensed milk on a medium heat (not too fierce or it will burn). Keep stirring until it is melted, then continue to cook until it becomes thick and a bit like fudge or toffee.
- Line the pastry case with the sliced bananas. Cover with the toffee base and allow to cool.
- Whip the cream and pour it over the cooled pie. Grate some plain chocolate over the top of the cream to garnish.
- Keep the pie in the fridge until you are ready to serve it.

Raspberry Trifle

Saucepan and serving bowl

6–8 trifle sponges (or break up some almost stale cake or muffins)

200g raspberries (you can use frozen)

600ml full fat milk

4 egg yolks

4 tablespoons cornflour

3 tablespoons sugar

1 teaspoon vanilla essence

200ml double or whipping cream

Raspberries to garnish

Toasted sliced almonds

- Arrange the sponges in the base of your trifle dish. If you like a boozy trifle, you can pour over some sherry or liqueur and let it soak into the sponge.
- Add the raspberries, ensuring they are pressed down around the sponge. It doesn't matter if you squelch the raspberries; it is nice to get some juice leaking into the sponge.
- Heat the milk until just below boiling point. While it is heating, mix the egg yolks, cornflour, sugar and vanilla essence together. Watch the milk to make sure it doesn't boil over.
- Remove the milk from the heat and add the egg mixture. Use a hand whisk and stir well.
- Return the mixture to the heat and continue to stir until the custard starts to thicken. Don't have the heat too high or it will burn.
- Once it has reached your desired thickness remove from the heat and leave to cool before pouring over the sponge and raspberries.
- Leave to cool. Whip the cream to a soft consistency and pour over the custard. Decorate the trifle with raspberries and toasted sliced almonds.

Summer Fruit Crumble

This is a great 'cheat' crumble. All you need is a pack of frozen summer fruits and some own-brand muesli or combo ingredients.

Ovenproof dish

400g frozen summer fruits
1–2 tablespoons sugar
75ml water

250–300g muesli
Brown sugar

- Preheat the oven to 180°C/gas mark 4.
- Place the summer fruits in the bottom of an ovenproof dish (no need to pre-cook if you don't want to!). Add 2 tablespoons water and a sprinkle of sugar if you have a sweet tooth.
- Cover with your crumble mix, finishing with a sprinkle of brown sugar. Bake in the oven for 15–20 minutes.

Variations
Here are some more ideas for great crumbles:

Rhubarb Crumble – I love rhubarb. You can make rhubarb crumble by cooking some fresh or frozen rhubarb in a pan with a little water. Or try mixing in some fresh strawberries to create a delicious **Strawberries and Rhubarb Crumble**, or some fresh or frozen raspberries to make a mouth-watering **Raspberry and Rhubarb Crumble**. Another great combo is **Rhubarb and Orange Crumble**. Add some orange segments alongside the rhubarb for a great citrus/rhubarb hit. If you like a bit of spice, try **Rhubarb and Ginger Crumble.**

Gooseberry and Elderflower Crumble – this is one of my favourites. Place prepared gooseberries in a saucepan with 2 tablespoons of elderflower cordial and 25g of sugar. Cook gently until the gooseberries just start to burst under pressure. Place in an ovenproof dish and cover with your crumble topping.

Pink Pears

This is a really simple dish and perfect to use up any stray pears in your fruit bowl.

Saucepan or slow cooker

4 pears, skinned

400ml apple juice

300ml red grape juice or red or mulled wine

200g raspberries, sieved

Juice and zest of 1 orange

1 teaspoon vanilla essence

50g sugar (optional, but needed if you have a sweet tooth)

1 cinnamon stick

To cook on the hob

• Peel the pears, retaining their stalks if you can. Lightly steam the whole skinned pears for 5 minutes.

• Meanwhile gently heat the apple and grape juice. Sieve the raspberries to remove the seeds and add the fruit to the apple and grape juice. Add the juice and zest of the orange, vanilla essence, sugar and cinnamon stick.

• Place the pears in the liquid and leave to heat gently for 30 minutes. Turn the pears occasionally to ensure they are fully covered in juice.

• Remove the cinnamon stick, arrange the pears in a dish and pour over the sauce. Serve with a dollop of low fat crème fraiche.

To cook in a slow cooker

• Preheat the slow cooker according to the manufacturer's instructions.

• Prepare the fruit as for the hob method, above, and add all the ingredients to the slow cooker. Turn the cooker to low and cook gently for 4–6 hours.

• Remove the cinnamon stick, arrange the pears in a dish and pour over the sauce. Serve with a dollop of low fat crème fraiche.

Note: This can be made in advance, allowing the flavours more time to be absorbed by the pears. Reheat gently prior to serving.

Steamed Chocolate Pudding

Pudding basin, slow cooker or steamer

150g butter	250g self-raising flour
160g sugar	50g cocoa
2 eggs	150ml milk
1 teaspoon vanilla essence	40g dark chocolate chips

- Beat the butter and sugar together until light and fluffy. Gradually add the eggs and vanilla essence.
- Sift the flour and cocoa together. Alternately add milk and sifted flour and cocoa to the egg and butter mixture until they are all well mixed together. Stir in the chocolate chips.
- Grease a 1.2 litre (2 pint) basin. Pour in the mixture. Cover with baking parchment and foil. Tie with string. Steam for 1½–2 hours.
- To cook in a slow cooker, place the pudding basin in the cooker and pour warm water into the cooker until it comes three-quarters of the way up the sides of the pudding basin. Turn the slow cooker to high and cook for 2–4 hours.
- Turn out the pudding onto a serving dish, and enjoy with a dollop of cream, ice cream or chocolate sauce.

Boozy Peach and Granola Pudding

This is a real grown-up dessert. You can create the same dish using any other fruits, so experiment.

Pudding basin and slow cooker

6–8 fresh peaches, sliced

125g brown sugar

75ml brandy

25g butter

2 teaspoons ground cinnamon

2 teaspoons vanilla extract

4–6 tablespoons granola

50g raisins

25g desiccated coconut

- Place the peach slices, sugar, brandy, butter, cinnamon and vanilla extract in an ovenproof dish (I use Pyrex) and mix well. Cover securely with foil.
- Turn your slow cooker to high. Place the dish in the slow cooker, and pour warm water into the cooker until it reaches halfway up the sides of the dish. Cook for 1–2 hours.
- Meanwhile combine the granola, raisins and coconut.
- Carefully remove the foil from the top of the dish. Sprinkle the granola mixture over the peach mixture. Do not re-cover, but make sure the water level around the dish is adequate.
- Continue to cook for another 30–50 minutes.
- Remove the dish and serve with a dollop of crème fraiche, yoghurt or ice cream.

Apple and Fruit Bread Pudding

This is a really easy dish to make, and avoids the need for the eggy custard the traditional puddings have. It is a bit of a cheat dish but very tasty – especially soothing on a cold winter's evening! As with all my puddings, serve with a dollop of low fat yoghurt or crème fraiche.

Saucepan and ovenproof dish

75g dried mixed fruit

1–2 teaspoons cinnamon

2–3 cooking apples, diced

150ml apple juice

125g stale/leftover bread, cut into small chunks

150ml milk

1–2 tablespoons brown sugar

- Preheat the oven to 180°C/gas mark 4.
- Put the dried fruit, cinnamon, apples and apple juice into a pan and bring to the boil for 5 minutes then remove from the heat.
- Stir in the bread and milk.
- Pour into a greased oven dish. Sprinkle over the brown sugar and bake in the oven for 25–30 minutes.

One Pot Conserves and Chutneys

Mum's Tomato Chutney

1kg ripe tomatoes, chopped

450g onions, chopped

2 garlic cloves, finely chopped

2 cooking apples, peeled, cored and chopped

2 teaspoons mustard seed or mustard powder

Small piece of fresh ginger (about 3cm long), grated

300g sultanas

200g light muscavado sugar

600ml spiced vinegar (malt will do if you cannot find ready spiced, or buy spices and spice your own)

Salt and pepper to taste

- Place all the ingredients (except the vinegar) in a preserving pan or large deep saucepan. Add half the vinegar and seasoning to taste .
- Place the pan over a medium heat and slowly bring to a simmer, stirring constantly until the sugar has dissolved.
- Simmer for 30–40 minutes, stirring often, until everything is tender.
- While the chutney is simmering, sterilise the jars. Wash them thoroughly in warm, clean, soapy water. Rinse and drain them upside down on kitchen towel and place on a baking tray or directly onto an oven rack (if directly onto the oven rack, take care when you remove them). Place in a preheated oven at 100°C/gas mark 1 for 15 minutes. Turn the oven down to its lowest setting to keep the jars warm while you make the chutney. When you remove the jars from the oven, place them onto an old newspaper or tea towel.
- Stir the remaining vinegar into the chutney and cook for a further 25 minutes or until it has thickened, stirring often. If it is still runny, simmer for another 10 minutes.
- Divide the chutney between the sterilised jars – I do this with a measuring jug – and allow to cool. Take care as it will be very hot and will splash as you fill the jars.
- When the chutney is cool place a waxed disc onto each jar and seal with airtight lids or cellophane and elastic bands. Store in a cool, dry place for a month to allow to mature. Once opened, store in the fridge and use within two months.

Mum's Spicy Chutney

Large saucepan or preserving pan and jars

1kg ripe tomatoes, chopped

450g of onions, chopped

2 garlic cloves, finely chopped

1 chilli, finely chopped (optional – add if you like it hot!)

2 cooking apples, peeled, cored and chopped

2 teaspoons mustard seed or mustard powder

Small piece of fresh ginger (about 3cm) long, grated

300g sultanas

200g light muscavado sugar

2 teaspoons chilli powder

2 teaspoons paprika

600ml spiced vinegar (malt will do if you cannot find ready spiced, or buy spices and spice your own)

Salt and pepper to taste

- Place all the ingredients (except the vinegar) in a preserving pan or large deep saucepan. Add half the vinegar and season to taste.
- Place the pan over a medium heat and slowly bring to a simmer, stirring constantly until the sugar has dissolved.
- Simmer for 30–40 minutes, stirring often, until everything is tender.
- While the chutney is simmering, sterilise the jars. Wash them thoroughly in warm, clean, soapy water. Rinse and drain them upside down on kitchen towel and place on a baking tray or directly onto an oven rack (if directly onto the oven rack, take care when you remove them). Place in a preheated oven at 100°C/gas mark 1 for 15 minutes. Turn the oven down to its lowest setting to keep the jars warm while you make the chutney. When you remove the jars from the oven, place them onto an old newspaper or tea towel.
- Stir the remaining vinegar into the chutney and cook for a further 25 minutes or until it has thickened, stirring often. If it is still runny, simmer for another 10 minutes.
- Divide the chutney between the sterilised jars – I do this with a measuring jug – and allow to cool. Take care as it will be very hot and will splash as you fill the jars.
- When the chutney is cool place a waxed disc onto each jar and seal with airtight lids or cellophane and elastic bands. Store in a cool, dry place for a month to allow to mature. Once opened, store in the fridge and use within two months.

Rhubarb and Ginger Chutney

Large saucepan or preserving pan and jars

1kg rhubarb, sliced
1 red onion, finely chopped
250g sultanas
12.5cm (5in) knuckle of ginger, finely chopped
400g brown sugar

75ml orange juice
400ml spiced vinegar or white malt vinegar
1 teaspoon curry powder
Salt and pepper to taste

- Place all the ingredients (except the vinegar) in a preserving pan or large deep saucepan. Add the vinegar and season to taste.
- Place the pan over a medium heat and slowly bring to a simmer, stirring constantly until the sugar has dissolved.
- Simmer for 40–50 minutes, stirring regularly until the mixture starts to thicken, otherwise it may stick.
- Prepare and sterilise the jars as instructed for **Mum's Tomato Chutney**, on page 231. Bottle the chutney and seal. Ideally, leave to mature for at least a month. Once opened, refrigerate and use within two months.

Mrs Green's Date Chutney

Mrs Green was our neighbour when I was growing up. When she moved into a retirement home when I was in my late teens, she gave me her wartime recipe notebook. I treasure it. It is full of amazing gems, the best of which will appear in many of my recipe books!

Large saucepan or preserving pan and jars

450g stoned dates

3 large onions, finely chopped

Juice and zest of 1 lemon

500ml vinegar

½ teaspoon cayenne pepper

1 teaspoon curry powder

2 teaspoons paprika

- Place all the ingredients in a pan and boil together for half an hour.
- Prepare and sterilise the jars, and bottle the chutney, as stated in **Mum's Tomato Chutney,** on page 231. Once opened, refrigerate and use within two months.

Spicy Mango Chutney

Large stock/preserving pan and jars

1.5kg mangoes, peeled and chopped

350ml water

75g brown sugar

75g raisins

2–3 cloves of garlic, crushed

1 cooking apple, diced

1 teaspoon cayenne pepper

1 stick of cinnamon

1 teaspoon coriander seeds

6 cloves

2 cardamom pods

2 bay leaves

45ml distilled vinegar

- Place the water and sugar in a stock/preserving pan and bring to the boil.
- Add all the remaining ingredients apart from the vinegar. Cover and reduce the heat to low.
- Cook for 20–25 minutes until the fruit is soft.
- Allow to cool, remove the bay leaves, cinnamon stick and cardamom pods before adding the vinegar.
- Prepare and sterilise the jars, and bottle the chutney, as stated in **Mum's Tomato Chutney**, on page 231. Once opened, refrigerate and use within one month.

Spicy Apricot Chutney

This is a really rich and spicy chutney, perfect to accompany curries or enliven your bread and cheese!

Large stock pan and jars

500g dried apricots

700g onions, finely chopped

2–3 cloves of garlic, crushed

1 teaspoon cayenne pepper

1 teaspoon paprika

1 teaspoon turmeric

2.5cm (1in) knuckle of fresh ginger, grated

750ml vinegar

200g sugar

250g sultanas

250g raisins

- Place the apricots in a bowl, cover with water and soak overnight.
- Drain the apricots and place in a large stock pan. Add all the remaining ingredients and cook on medium heat for approximately 1 hour. The chutney should be smooth but not too runny.
- Prepare and sterilise the jars, and bottle the chutney, as instructed in **Mum's Tomato Chutney**, on page 231. Once opened, refrigerate and use within one month.

Slow Cook Fruit and Chilli Chutney

Saucepan, slow cooker and jars

600g red onions, finely chopped

600g Bramley apples, peeled and chopped

200g pears, peeled and chopped

200g plums, peeled and chopped

150g sultanas

50g fresh ginger, finely chopped

2–3 chillies (depending on your personal taste)

750g sugar

450ml white wine vinegar

- This is ideal if your slow cooker base can also be used on the hob; if not, you will have to use a saucepan to start, then transfer to your slow cooker.
- Turn your slow cooker to high. Place all the ingredients in the saucepan or slow cooker base (if hob proof). Bring to the boil and simmer for 5 minutes.
- Transfer to your slow cooker (if necessary) and cook on high for 4 hours, until the mixture has reduced by half.
- When you have achieved the right consistency, bottle in sterilised jars (see **Mum's Tomato Chutney** recipe on page 231 for full details of how to sterilise the jars). Cover with waxed paper and store for at least 1 month. Once opened, refrigerate and use within two months.

Red Onion Marmalade

This is a huge favourite of mine. Delicious served with cheese on toast, or why not uses this as your base for a red onion and goats' cheese tart. You can cook this in a casserole dish, preserving pan or slow cooker.

Casserole dish, preserving pan or slow cooker and jars

2–3 tablespoons of olive oil
450g red onions, sliced
20g butter
3 tablespoons dark brown sugar
50g sultanas

1 teaspoon paprika
200ml red wine
40ml balsamic vinegar
Seasoning to taste

To cook on the hob
- Heat the oil in a casserole dish. Add the onions and butter and cook until the onions are soft and translucent.
- Add the sugar and stir well. Cover and leave on a low heat for 15 minutes to start to caramelise.
- Add the remaining ingredients. Cook for another 30 minutes or until the marmalade liquid has reduced, but not dried. Season to taste.
- Prepare and sterilise the jars, and bottle the chutney, as instructed in **Mum's Tomato Chutney**, on page 231. Once opened, refrigerate and use within two months.

To cook in a slow cooker
- Preheat your slow cooker as recommended in your manufacturer's instructions.
- Heat the oil in a sauté pan or the base of your slow cooker. I use my Crock-Pot so I can switch from hob heat back to the slow cooker base without using another pan.
- Add the onions and the butter. Cook until the onions are soft and translucent.
- Add the sugar and stir well. If you have been cooking on the hob, transfer to your slow cooker. Turn the cooker to hot and leave for 1 hour.
- Add the remaining ingredients and leave for another 2 hours.
- Add seasoning to taste – you may want to add more sugar or balsamic vinegar to suit your palate. Cook for another 30 minutes or until the marmalade liquid has reduced, but not dried.
- Prepare and sterilise the jars, and bottle the chutney, as instructed in **Mum's Tomato Chutney**, on page 231. Once opened, refrigerate and use within two months.

Green Tomato Chutney

This recipe is perfect for using up those tomatoes that are green at the end of the season. You can halve the ingredients in this recipe if you prefer to make less.

Large saucepan or preserving pan and jars

900g green tomatoes, chopped	7.5cm (3in) knuckle of fresh ginger, finely
6 large onions, chopped	chopped
225g sugar	1 pepper, finely chopped
225g sultanas	1 litre of vinegar
10g cloves	1 teaspoon grated nutmeg
1 teaspoon mace	3–5 chillies, depending on taste, finely chopped

- Place all the ingredients in a preserving pan and stir well. Stew gently for 2½ to 3 hours. You can do this in a slow cooker on high if you prefer.
- Once the chutney has reached the desired thickness, prepare the jars, sterilise and bottle as directed in **Mum's Tomato Chutney** on page 231. Use within one month.

Marrow Chutney

Large saucepan or preserving pan and jars

500g marrow flesh

½ lemon

225g sugar

300g cooking apples

5cm (2in) knuckle of fresh ginger, finely cut

150g sultanas

400ml pickling vinegar

- Remove the flesh from the marrow, dice into small pieces and place in a preserving pan.
- Place the zest of the lemon in the pan, and then carefully remove any remaining pith (white parts of the lemon) before chopping the lemon into small pieces and adding to the pan.
- Add all the remaining ingredients to the preserving pan. Bring to the boil and cook slowly for 1–1½ hours, stirring as often as possible.
- When the chutney has reached the desired consistency, prepare the jars, sterilise and bottle as instructed in **Mum's Tomato Chutney** on page 231.
- Store in the fridge and, once opened, use within two months.

Slow Cook Fruity Chutney

If you have some overripe fruit, instead of throwing it away, why not turn it into a tasty chutney? Combine these ingredients in your slow cooker for a simple, yet delicious, chutney. Alternatively, if you prefer, you can cook this on the hob in a preserving pan.

Slow cooker or preserving pan and jars

3 onions, finely chopped	50g raisins
3–4 cloves garlic, crushed	200g sugar
7.5cm (3in) knuckle of fresh ginger, grated	1 teaspoon ground cinnamon
3 ripe peaches, chopped	1 teaspoon allspice
3 ripe pears, chopped	4 teaspoons wholegrain mustard
2 apples, chopped	500ml vinegar
200g sultanas	

To cook in a slow cooker

- Preheat the slow cooker according to the manufacturer's instructions.
- Place all the ingredients in your slow cooker. Turn to low and cook for 5–6 hours, until the mixture is the right consistency.
- Prepare and sterilise your jars and bottle the chutney as instructed in **Mum's Tomato Chutney** recipe on page 231.
- Store in the fridge and, once opened, use within two months.

To cook in a preserving pan

- If you prefer to cook this in a preserving pan, place all the ingredients in the pan and cook on medium heat for 1 hour before bottling in your sterilised jars.
- Store in the fridge and, once opened, use within one month.

Slow Cook Cranberry Sauce

You'll really get into the Christmas spirit if you make this amazing sauce; the whole house will smell wonderfully Christmassy.

Slow cooker

400g cranberries

1 cooking apple, finely sliced

250ml orange juice

200g sugar

2–3 teaspoons ground cinnamon

- Preheat the slow cooker according to the manufacturer's instructions.
- Place all the ingredients in the slow cooker and stir well to ensure everything is well blended. Turn the cooker to high and cook for 3–4 hours, stirring occasionally.
- Pour into a serving dish or into sterilised jars (see instructions for sterilising in **Mum's Tomato Chutney** recipe on page 231) until you are ready to use. Once opened, refrigerate and use within one month.

Pomegranate Molasses

This is great as a marinade. You can buy it in bottles from specialist shops – it is popular in Lebanese or Moroccan stores – or from specialist delis. But it's so easy to make, why not have a go and bottle it ready for use?

Large saucepan or preserving pan and jars

750ml pomegranate Juice

100g sugar

250ml lemon juice

- Place all the ingredients in a pan and simmer gently until the liquid has reduced by at least half.
- Use immediately or bottle in a sterilised jar (see **Mum's Tomato Chutney** recipe on page 231 for full instructions) until required. This will keep for up to six months if bottled in a sterilised jar.

Orange and Lemon Marmalade

Large saucepan or preserving pan and jars

15 oranges (Seville are traditionally the best)	4 litres of water
3 lemons	1.5kg sugar

- Extract the juice from the oranges and lemons. I use my electric citrus juicer for this as it is quick and easy, and retains the pulp and flesh (which we need).
- Pour the juice into a preserving pan. Keep the pulp and the pips in a bowl, and now focus on the peel.
- Chop the peel into shreds. I prefer fine shreds, but do this to suit your own preference. Once chopped, add this to the juice in the preserving pan, along with the water.
- Scoop up the pulp and pips and place them in a muslin bag. Tie the bag tightly and add it to the preserving pan, making sure it is submerged in the juice.
- Bring to the boil and simmer gently until the peel is tender. This can take anything from 45 minutes to over an hour. Once you are happy with the peel, carefully remove the muslin bag. This will be very hot so be careful. Leave to cool slightly in a bowl (so you don't waste any juice that may seep out). Once it is cooler, you can squeeze out the excess juice and return it to the preserving pan.
- Add the sugar, and bring to the boil. Remove any scum from the surface of the mixture. You are now waiting for the jam to start to set. Check this after 15 minutes, then every 10 minutes until you are happy. To check, spoon a little of the mixture onto a saucer. Leave to cool (or place in the fridge if you are in a hurry). If it forms a skin, it is done and ready to bottle.
- Prepare the jars, sterilise them and bottle the marmalade according to the instructions given for **Mum's Tomato Chutney** on page 231. Top each jar with with a waxed paper disc, cover and store until needed.

Mrs Green's Dried Apricot Jam

This is another of Mrs Green's gems. It's a very simple recipe.

Large saucepan or preserving pan and jars

450g dried apricots

1.5 litres of water

About 1kg sugar

- Soak the apricots in the water for 48 hours.
- Boil the fruit and water for 1½ hours. Add the sugar (340g sugar for every 500ml of water) and boil for 1 hour.
- Prepare and sterilise the jars as instructed in **Mum's Tomato Chutney** on page 231 and bottle as required.

Mrs Green's Gooseberry Jam

Again, this is from my childhood neighbour Mrs Green's wartime notebook. It makes a wonderful jam and is a real favourite in our house.

Large saucepan or preserving pan and jars

450g sugar

250ml water

450g gooseberries

- Boil the sugar and water together for 15 minutes. Add the gooseberries and simmer gently until the jam is clear and set.
- Prepare and sterilise the jars as instructed in **Mum's Tomato Chutney** on page 231 and bottle as required. If stored in sterile jars and sealed correctly this should keep for several months.

Mum's Fabulous Raspberry Jam

This recipe makes around 2.7kg of jam.

Large saucepan or preserving pan and jars

1.8kg raspberries

1.8kg sugar (Mum uses half granulated sugar and half jam sugar)

- Wash and dry the jam jars and put into a warm oven to sterilise (see **Mum's Tomato Chutney** recipe on page 231 for full instructions).
- Wash the fruit if necessary and drain well. Place in a preserving pan.
- Simmer until some juice has been extracted.
- Add the sugar, stirring until it has dissolved.
- Bring to the boil and boil rapidly for 5–10 minutes until the jam sets when tested.
- Test by putting a little jam onto a cold saucer and leaving for a few minutes. If it creases when you run your finger across it, the jam is ready.
- Remove the scum and leave the jam to cool slightly.
- Pot and seal while still warm. If stored in sterile jars and sealed correctly this should last for several months.

Mum's Raspberry and Redcurrant Jam

This recipe makes around 2.7kg of jam.

Large saucepan or preserving pan and jars

900g raspberries

900g redcurrants

1.8kg sugar (Mum uses half granulated sugar and half jam sugar)

- Wash and dry the jam jars and put into a warm oven to sterilise (see **Mum's Tomato Chutney** recipe on page 231 for full instructions).
- Wash the fruit if necessary and drain well. Place in a preserving pan.
- Simmer until some juice has been extracted.
- Add the sugar, stirring until it has dissolved.
- Bring to the boil and boil rapidly for 5–10 minutes until the jam sets when tested.
- Test by putting a little jam onto a cold saucer and leaving for a few minutes. If it creases when you run your finger across it, the jam is ready.
- Remove the scum and leave the jam to cool slightly.
- Pot and seal while still warm. If stored in sterile jars and sealed correctly this should last for several months.

Contacts and Further Information

In this chapter you will find further information about the equipment used in the recipes in this book, as well as contact details for manufacturers. All the details given were correct at the time of going to press. You can often find bargain slow cookers and one pot dishes in supermarkets.

Slow cookers

Before buying a slow cooker, decide exactly what features you need. You may want a timer facility, especially if you are out at work all day and don't have any way of turning off or monitoring the cooking. Alternatively, you could invest in a timer plug, though the disadvantage of this is that you won't have a keep warm option. What size cooker do you need? If there are only two of you, you may decide a smaller capacity cooker is adequate but, if you want to experiment with baking cakes or desserts, or cooking whole joints or large cuts of meat, a larger one may be more suitable. Opting for a clear lid can enable you to see the food without lifting the lid. Do you want a sauté facility? If so, this may be a crock-pot that can be used on a hob or even placed under the grill. Think carefully about what you need and how it will be used before buying. I own two slow cookers – one for sweet dishes and the other for savoury. It sounds extravagant but once you get the slow cook bug it is hard to revert back to more traditional ways of cooking, especially when you are busy.

Which? Reviewed slow cookers and their five best buys were as follows:

Cuisinart CSC650U came top, scoring 77%. This is quite an expensive machine at £75, but looks very stylish and functions well. It comes with a massive five-year guarantee, which offers great peace of mind. Unlike most slow cookers, it is square in shape, but with a 4.5 litre capacity, it is perfect for families. It has a warm facility which is very useful and ensures that the meal does not spoil.

Breville VTP043 came a close second, scoring 75%, and at £30, less than half the price of the Cuisinart, it has to be a real bargain. It has a 5.5 litre capacity and comes with a year's guarantee, a glass lid, and auto, low and high facility.

Breville VTP062 scored 74%, and is slightly more expensive than the previous Breville at £38. It is an oval shape with a capacity of 4 litres. it has a glass lid, auto, low and hot settings and comes with a year's guarantee.

Morphy Richards 48724 scored well with 73%. Priced at £60, it has a lovely shape (a bit like a witch's cauldron). It has digital display, glass lid, low, high and warm settings and a 3 litre capacity. It also comes with a two-year guarantee.

Morphy Richards Intellichef 4880 is £130, but scored 73% in the Which? review. It is the most expensive of the top five, but it does have many functions, such as slow cook, steam, bake, boil, shallow fry, rice-cook, warm, and it also reheats food. It also uses less energy than other slow cookers. It has a 3 litre capacity and comes with a two-year guarantee.

My personal favourite – and the one in which I cooked most of the recipes in this book – is the **Crock-Pot® Sauté Slow Cooker**. You can use the removable Stoneware cooking pot directly on the heat, which is perfect for when your recipe needs you to brown meat, sauté vegetables or even caramelise fruit. You then add the remaining ingredients and return the Stoneware pot to the heating cradle to continue to cook the meal in the usual slow way. The Stoneware can also be used in a conventional oven and if you have any leftovers, you can store them in the freezer. The cooker is available in 4.7 litre or 6.7 litre capacity. The latter has a timer which automatically switches to keep warm facility when the end of the cooking time is reached. Call 0800 0523615 for stockist information.

Morphy Richards If you are looking for a green option, the **Morphy Richards Ecolectric Slow Cooker** claims to have green credentials, though I am not clear if they are comparing it to conventional cooking or other slow cookers.

JML's Direct's Star Chef, a slow cooker that uses ceramic technology for maximum heat distribution, has an automatic keep-warm function, and electronic LCD digital display makes it easy to choose and select the mode and time you need. The Star Chef retails at £99.99, so is a little more expensive than other slow cookers. For more information, visit www.JMLdirect.com or call 0871 2222 631.

Lakeland There is not much that Lakeland don't offer. They seem to think of all the kitchen equipment we need and dream of. I would recommend the **Prestige® Family 4.5 litre Slow Cooker**, £49.99, and **Lakeland's 3.5 Litre Slow Cooker**, £29.99. Both have a ceramic pot and three settings – Low for simmering and slow cooking; High for faster cooking; and Auto, which regulates temperature automatically. Both also have a glass lid that lets you keep an eye on proceedings.

Casserole dishes

One pot and casserole dishes are widely available. I prefer to use Pyrex or cast-iron dishes as I can use these on the hob, in the oven, and to serve from. This saves on washing up and means I don't have to worry about whether a dish will crack on direct contact with the heat. The following are some of the best:

Le Creuset I am a massive fan of the entire range. My Le Creuset sauté pan and casserole dishes are used almost daily. You may pay slightly more for Le Creuset, but they are very well made, will last for years and are a really good investment. Available in a range of great colours, they will certainly brighten up your kitchen. Products come with either a 10-year or a lifetime guarantee. Visit www.lecreuset.co.uk or call 0800 37 37 92 for more information.

Pyrex You can't go wrong with Pyrex. They are durable and perfect for a wide range of uses. They come out gleaming from the dishwasher time after time. I have recently been converted to the new Pyroflam® range. Pyroflam® is made of Vitro-Ceramic®, a material so resistant that it was first used by NASA in the conception of space shuttles. It is supposed to withstand extreme temperature changes, which means you can literally take it from the freezer and place it straight in the oven or on a hob. It also comes with a 25-year guarantee. Pyrex is available from Amazon, Lakeland, John Lewis and a wide range of cook shops, departments stores and supermarkets.

Tefal® WiKook Fast Cooker With its patented Power Lid, Tefal's new WiKook seals in heat and low pressure to prepare dishes up to 25% faster than traditional cooking, retaining more vitamins and minerals for healthier, tastier meals. And, unlike most ordinary pressure cookers, the lid can be opened at any time during cooking to stir, taste or add ingredients. The 4mm thick aluminium base ensures even heat distribution and the non-stick surface means clean-up is painless. Suitable for all hobs (including induction).

JML Direct offer some great homeware bargains. I can highly recommend the Halogen Oven (much faster and cheaper to run than using a conventional oven). If you are looking for a cast-iron casserole dish but can't afford the cost of a Le Creuset, you could opt for JML's Country Cookware, which comes with a 25-year guarantee and is available as a complete set or you can just buy the casserole dish. For more information, visit www.JMLdirect.com or call 0871 2222 631.

Typhoon Housewares sell a wide range of homeware, including great casserole dishes such as The Stockholm Triple Casserole dish. For more information visit www.typhoonhousewares.co.uk

Index

(v) indicates recipe suitable for vegetarians